...nuting Closer closer closer to you Closer closer closer to round your bed Right...

...am to you I attempt everyday Closer closer closer to you If I had my wishes...

...time you were around I'd view you walking by Closer Wish I was a ticking...

If I was a pair of boots I wouldn't have to beg I'd be closer closer to you Closer...

...my Wishes warm cups I pretend that I'm a sled to satisfied Just being round...

...get closer closer to you If I was a necklace Hanging decorate your lips Closer...

...once when you leave Wish I was a velvet shirt Draped down your front Wishing...

...nuting Closer closer closer to you Closer closer closer to round your bed Right...

The Merchant of Venice

莎翁戏剧经典

威尼斯商人

〔英〕威廉·莎士比亚　著
张文庭　注释

商務印書館
SINCE 1897　The Commercial Press
2016年·北京

威廉·莎士比亚

图 1（见 4 页）

Venice. A street.

Enter ANTONIO, SALARION, *and* SOLANIO.

ANTONIO.

...

And such a want-wit sadness makes of me,
That I have much ado to know myself.

SALARINO.

...

Do overpeer the petty traffickers,
That curtsey to them, do them reverence,
As they fly by them with their woven wings.

SOLANIO.

...

And every object that might make me fear
Misfortune to my ventures, out of doubt
Would make me sad.

图 2（见 44 页）

Belmont. A room in PORTIA'S *house.*

Enter the PRINCE OF MOROCCO, a tawny Moor, *all in white, and three or four* FOLLOWERS accordingly, with PORTIA, NERISSA, *and their* TRAIN. *flourish of cornets.*

PRINCE OF MOROCCO.

...

I tell thee, lady, this aspect of mine
Hath fear'd the valiant: ...

图 3（见 50 页）

OLD GOBBO.

By God's sonties, 'twill be a hard way to hit. …

LAUNCELOT GOBBO

Talk you of young Master Launcelot?

图 4（见 52 页）

LAUNCELOT GOBBO.

Do you not know me，father?

OLD GOBBO.

Alack，sir，I am sand-blind；I know you not.

图 5（见 66 页）

The same. A street.

Enter GRATIANO, LORENZO, SALARINO, *and* SOLANIO.

LORENZO.

Nay, we will slink away in supper-time,
Disguise us at my lodging, and return
All in an hour.

GRATIANO.

We have not made good preparation.

图 6（见 74 页）

JESSICA.

Farewell; and if my fortune be not crost,
I have a father, you a daughter, lost. [*Exit*.

图 7（见 74 页）

The same.

Enter the maskers GRATIANO *and* SALARINO.

GRATIANO.

And it is marvel he out-dwells his hour,
For lovers ever run before the clock.

SALARINO.

O, ten times faster Venus' pigeons fly
...
To keep obliged faith unforfeited!

图 8（见 80 页）

ANTONIO.

Fie, fie, Gratiano! Where are all the rest?
'Tis nine o'clock; our friends all stay for you.

...

GRATIANO.

I am glad on't: I desire no more delight
Than to be under sail and gone to-night.

图 9（见 88 页）

SOLANIO.
I never heard a passion so confused,
So strange, outrageous, and so variable,
As the dog Jew did utter in the streets:
...

图 **10**（见 96 页）

SERVENT.

Yet I have not seen

...

So likely an ambassador of love：
A day in April never came so sweet，
To show how costly summer was at hand，
As this fore-spurrer comes before his lord.

图 **11**（见 100 页）

Venice. A street.

Enter SOLANIO *and* SALARINO.

SOLANIO.

...

—Why, the end is, he hath lost a ship.

SALARINO.

I would it might prove the end of his losses.

图 12（见 108 页）

TUBAL.

There came divers of Antonio's creditors in my company
To Venice, that swear he cannot choose but break.

SHYLOCK.

I am very glad of it:—I'll plague him; I'll torture him:—I am glad on't.

图 **13**（见 132—134 页）

Venice. A street.

Enter SHYLOCK, SALARINO, ANTONIO, *and* GAOLER.

SHYLOCK.

I'll have my bond; speak not against my bond:
I have sworn an oath that I will have my bond.

图 14（见 150 页）

Venice. A court of justice.

Enter the DUKE, *the* MAGNIFICOES, ANTONIO, BASSANIO, GRATIANO, SOLANIO, SALARINO, *and* others.

DUKE OF VENICE.

What, is Antonio here?

ANTONIO.

Ready, so please your Grace.

DUKE OF VENICE.

I am sorry for thee: thou art come to answer
A stony adversary, an inhuman wretch
Uncapable of pity; void and empty
From any dram of mercy.

图 15（见 162 页）

Enter PORTIA *for* BALTHAZAR.

PORTIA.

... I am informed thoroughly of the cause.—
Which is the merchant here, and which the Jew?

图 16（见 180 页）

SHYLOCK.

You take my life,

...

When you to take the means whereby I live.

图 17（见 186 页）

GRATIANO.

Fair sir, you are well o'erta'en:
My Lord Bassanio, upon more advice,
Hath sent you here his ring; and doth entreat
Your company at dinner.

图 18（见 190 页）

Belmont. Avenue to PORTIA'S *house.*

Enter LORENZO *and* JESSICA.

JESSICA.

In such a night
Medea gather'd the enchanted herbs
That did renew old Aeson.

LORENZO.

In such a night
Did Jessica steal form the wealthy Jew,
And with an unthrift love did run from Venice
As far as Belmont.

“莎翁戏剧经典”丛书总序

莎士比亚(William Shakespeare, 1564—1616)是英国16世纪文艺复兴时期的伟大剧作家和诗人,也是世界文坛上的巨擘。他一生创作了38部戏剧作品(一说37部),诗作包括两部长篇叙事诗、一部十四行诗集以及其他一些短篇诗作。四百多年来这些作品被翻译成多种文字,在世界各地广泛传播。正如他同时代的批评家和剧作家本·琼生所说,他是“时代的灵魂”,“不属一个时代,而属于所有的时代!”莎士比亚在世期间,他的戏剧作品曾吸引了大量观众,包括宫廷王室成员和普通百姓,产生了巨大影响。18世纪以来,这些作品始终活跃在舞台上,20世纪随着电影业的发展,它们又被搬上银幕。几百年来,无论是体现莎士比亚原作的表演还是经过不断改编的作品,莎剧都拥有众多的观者,散发出不灭的艺术光辉;另一方面,自1623年莎士比亚全集第一对开本问世,莎士比亚的戏剧也成为学者和广大普通读者阅读、学习、研究的对象,在历代读者的阅读和研究中,这些作品不断得到新阐释和挖掘。莎士比亚的作品焕发着永久不衰的生命活力。

1564年4月,莎士比亚出生于英格兰中部的埃文河畔的斯特拉福镇。家境殷实,父亲曾经营手套和羊毛,并做过小镇的镇长。莎士比亚小时曾在镇上的文法学校读书,受到过较为正规的拉丁文和古典文学的教育。不久,家道中落,陷入经济困境,这可能成为莎士比亚后来未能进入大学读书的原因。1582年,莎士比亚十八岁时与邻村一位大他八岁的女子安·哈撒韦成婚,六个月后,大女儿苏珊娜降生,此后他们又有了一对孪生子女,不幸的是,儿子哈姆内特早夭。16世纪90年代左右,莎士比亚来到伦敦,发展他的戏剧事业。他曾是剧团的演员、编剧和股东。90年代初期,莎士比亚即开始戏剧创作。1592年,莎士比亚已在同行中崭露头角,被当时的"大学才子"剧作家格林所嫉妒,他把莎士比亚称作"那只新抖起来的乌鸦","借我们的羽毛来打扮自己……狂妄地幻想着能独自震撼(Shake-scene)这个国家的舞台"。1592—1594年间,伦敦因流行瘟疫,大部分剧院关闭,在此期间莎士比亚完成了两部著名的长篇叙事诗《维纳斯与阿多尼斯》与《鲁克丽丝受辱记》。1594年剧院恢复营业之后,莎士比亚加入宫廷大臣剧团,并终生服务于该剧团,直到1613年离开伦敦返回家乡。90年代中期,他进入了戏剧创作的巅峰时期。在1590年至1613年的二十多年之间,莎士比亚共创作了历史剧、悲剧、喜剧、传奇剧等38部。90年代中后期,他的创作以喜剧和历史剧为主,包括喜剧《仲夏夜之梦》(1595)、《威尼斯商人》(1596)、《无事生非》(1598—1599)、《皆大欢喜》(1599—1600)等和大部分历史剧,如《理查三世》(1592—1593)、《亨利四世》(上、下)(1596—1598)、《亨利五世》(1598—1599)等。这一时期,他的创作风格较为明快,充满积极向上的格调,即便剧中有悲剧的成分,整个作品也透露出对生活的肯定,对理想的向往,如《罗密欧与朱丽叶》(1595)。进入17世纪后,莎士比亚的戏剧更多地转向对人生重大问题的思考,探索解决人生之困顿的途径,诸如权力、欲望、嫉妒、暴政等等。四大悲剧《哈姆莱特》(1600—1601)、《奥瑟罗》(1603—1604)、《李尔王》(1605—1606)、《麦克白》(1606)均完成于这一时期。此外,几部重要的罗马题材剧也在90年代末和新世纪的最初几年完成,如《裘力·凯撒》(1599)、《安东尼与克里奥佩特拉》(1606)、《科里奥兰纳斯》(1608)等。莎士比亚这一时期也创作了几部喜剧,但风格较前一时期更多悲情色彩,更为沉重而引人深思。1609年,莎士比亚《十四行诗集》出版。晚期的莎士比亚剧作风格有一定变化,最有影响的是传奇剧,如《暴风雨》,通过想象的世界与现实世界的对照来探讨人生问题。

莎士比亚的名字开始传入中国是在19世纪中上叶,他的戏剧被翻译成汉语而为国人所知则是在20世纪初期。当时,他剧作的内容通过英国19世纪兰姆姐弟《莎士比亚戏剧故事集》的汉译被介绍到中国来，即无译者署名的《澥外奇谭》(1903)和林纾、魏易翻译的《吟边燕语》(1904)。20世纪20年代，莎剧汉译事业的开拓者田汉翻译了《哈孟雷特》(1921)和《罗密欧与朱丽叶》(1924)。此后，朱生豪、梁实秋、孙大雨、曹禺、曹未风、虞尔昌等译家都翻译过莎士比亚的剧作。朱生豪先生在经历日本侵略的苦难、贫穷和疾病折磨的极其艰苦的环境下，以惊人的毅力和顽强的意志，克服种种艰难险阻，穷毕生之精力完成了31部半莎剧的翻译，成为播撒莎士比亚文明之火的普罗米修斯，译莎事业的英雄和圣徒。他的莎剧译文优美畅达，人物性格鲜明，成为广大读者所珍爱的艺术瑰宝。梁实秋是中国迄今为止唯一一位个人独立完成莎剧和莎诗汉译工程的翻译家。梁译有详尽的注释和说明，学术含量较高。1956年，卞之琳翻译的《哈姆雷特》出版，他完善了孙大雨提出的翻译原则，提出"以顿代步、韵式依原诗、等行翻译"的翻译方法，可谓开一代诗体译法之风，他的译本至今都被视作该剧最优秀的译本。方平是另一位重要的成绩卓著的莎剧翻译家。2000年由他主编主译的《新莎士比亚全集》出版，其中25部莎剧由方平翻译，其他作品由阮坤、吴兴华、汪义群、覃学岚、屠岸、张冲等译出，为国内目前首部全部由分行诗体翻译的莎剧莎诗全集。

时至今日，莎士比亚的戏剧作品仍不断有新的译本出版，对广大读者而言，阅读汉译的莎剧已经是一件十分方便的事情，而这些汉译莎剧作品中不乏优秀的译本。然而，尽管莎剧的汉译丰富多彩，莎剧的改编层出不穷，要想真正了解莎剧的本来面目，我们还需要回到莎剧原文本身。其中的原因有三：一、每一种语言都是丰富的，其表达的意义可能是多元多面的，但由于译出语和译入语两种语言之间的差异，再好的翻译也只能尽可能地贴近原文而不可能百分之百地再现原文的魅力，因此，阅读再好的译本也无法取代或等同于阅读原作；二、莎士比亚生活的时代距今已经有约400年，他所使用的英语与今天人们所熟悉的英语已有较大差异，当时的人们所熟悉的文化和历史事件也是我们今天并不熟知的，因此，要真正领悟他的作品，还需回到他那时的语言和文化中去；三、莎剧经过约400年的变迁，在改编中不断变换，有些已经走出了莎士比亚时代的莎剧，因而，想要认识和了解莎剧，最佳的办法还是回到莎剧的原文本中去。

莎士比亚生活和创作的时期在16世纪末17世纪初。英语在当时已经得到极大的发展，十分活跃而成熟，尤其莎士比亚戏剧中所运用的英语，文辞丰富、结构灵活、表达力很强。但随着时代的发展，其中的一些用词、用语以及语义等都发生了变化，与我们今天的英语存在一定距离，理解起来也就会有一定困难。莎剧在绝大多数情况下采用的是诗体写作，即人物的语言是分行的，每行十个音节，轻重音节相间，一轻一重的每两个音节构成一个音步，不押韵，因此，他的剧作均为抑扬格五音步的素体诗。这样的诗体形式突显出莎剧语言的艺术魅力，音韵优美、铿锵，节奏感强，表达生动有力。然而，正因为这是诗体写作，在语法上就可能出现诗语言特有的结构，比如倒装句或词序颠倒的现象等。莎剧的语言丰富多彩，不同人物的话语呈现出多种特色，时而体现出古典拉丁语的文风，时而出现双关语、俚语、隐喻等修辞手法。典故、历史事件、政治元素、宗教、生活习俗等等都可能成为今天的读者理解莎剧原文本的障碍。因而，借助良好的注释来理解莎剧的原作就成为我们了解和认识莎剧原貌的必要手段。这次由商务印书馆隆重推出的“莎翁戏剧经典”丛书，重点选出莎士比亚的12部经典剧作，在裘克安先生主编的“莎士比亚注释”丛书的基础上进行了改编修订，并加入了精美的插图。裘先生主编的“莎士比亚注释”丛书对莎剧原文做了多方面的详尽注释，对理解原文起到有效作用，在读者中有较广泛的影响。相信这套“莎翁戏剧经典”的出版会进一步推动莎剧在广大读者中的影响力，提高人们对阅读莎剧以及经典文学作品原文的兴趣和能力，产生积极的和广泛的影响。

屠岸 章燕

2013年10月4日

“莎士比亚注释”丛书总序

莎士比亚研究在新中国有过不平坦的道路和坎坷的命运。解放后不久，大家纷纷学俄语，学英语的人数骤减。研究英国文学，要看苏联人怎么说。“文革”十年，莎士比亚同其他西方“资产阶级”作家一样被打入冷宫。改革开放以后，1978 年人民文学出版社出版了在朱生豪译文基础上修订补足的《莎士比亚全集》。随之又出版了一些个别剧的不同译本，如方平译的《莎士比亚喜剧五种》(1979 年)和卞之琳译的《莎士比亚悲剧四种》(1988 年)。梁实秋的译本，现在大陆上也可以读到了。评介和研究莎士比亚的文章，从“文革”结束后才逐渐多起来。

但是，目前多数人学习、欣赏和研究莎士比亚，是通过中译文来进行的。精通英语而研究莎士比亚的学者不是没有，然而他们人数不多，年纪却老迈了。最近若干年，才有一些年轻人到英国或美国去学习和研究莎士比亚。

1981 年我就想到有必要在中国出版我们自己注释的莎士比亚著作。谈起来，许多朋友都赞成。1984 年中国莎士比亚研究会筹备和成立时，我自告奋勇，联系了一些志同道合的学者，共同开始编写莎士比亚注释本。商务印书馆大力支持出版这套丛书。到 2002 年底已出书 26 种，而且第一次印刷版已全部售完。这证明这套丛书是很受欢迎的。

要知道，莎士比亚是英语文学中最优秀的代表人物，他又是英语语言大师，学习、欣赏和研究他的原著，是译文无法替代的。商务印书馆以其远见卓识，早在 1910 年和 1921—1935 年间，就出版过几种莎士比亚剧本的注释本，以满足这方面的需求。那时的教会学校学生英文水平高，能读莎著；不但大学生能读，连有些中学生都能读。可从那时以后，整整 50 年中国就没印过原文的莎士比亚著作。

世界各国，莎著的注释本多得不计其数。如果唯独中国没有，实在说不过去。如果没有，对于中国知识分子欣赏和研究莎士比亚十分不利。近年来，中国人学英语的越来越多了，他们的英文水平也逐渐提高了。因此，也存在着一定的读者市场。

有了注释本，可以为明天的莎士比亚研究提供一个可靠的群众基础。而译本显然不能提供可靠的基础。

莎士比亚是16、17世纪之交的作者，他写的又是诗剧。对于现代的读者，他的英语呈现着不少的困难。不要说掌握了现代英语的中国读者，就是受过一般教育的英美人士，在初读莎士比亚原著时也面临许多障碍，需要注释的帮助。

莎士比亚的时代，英语正从受屈折变化拘束的中世纪英语，向灵活而丰富的现代英语转变。拉丁语和法语当时对英语影响很大。而莎士比亚对英语的运用又有许多革新和创造。主要的困难可以归纳为以下几个方面，也就是注释要提供帮助的方面：

（一）词汇。许多词虽然拼法和现在一样，但具有不同的早期含义，不能望文生义。另有一些词拼法和现在不一样，而含义却相同。莎士比亚独创了一些词。他特别喜欢用双关语，在他创作的早期尤其如此。而双关语是无从翻译的。这是译本无论如何也代替不了注释本的原因之一。

让我们举《哈姆莱特》剧中男主角出场后最初讲的几句话为例：

King: But now, my cousin Hamlet, and my son —
Hamlet 〔Aside〕: A little more than kin, and less than kind!
King: How is it that the clouds still hang on you?
Hamlet: Not so, my lord. I am too much i' the sun.

• 梁实秋的译文如下：

王：现在，我的侄子哈姆雷特，也是我的儿子，——
哈[旁白]：比侄子是亲些，可是还算不得儿子。
王：怎么，你脸上还是罩着一层愁云？
哈：不是的，陛下；我受的阳光太多了。

• 卞之琳的译文如下：

王：得，哈姆雷特，我的侄子，我的儿——

哈[旁白]：亲上加亲，越亲越不相亲！

王：你怎么还是让愁云惨雾罩着你？

哈：陛下，太阳大，受不了这个热劲"儿"。

• 朱生豪的译文如下：

王：可是来，我的侄儿哈姆莱特，我的孩子——

哈[旁白]：超乎寻常的亲族，漠不相干的路人。

王：为什么愁云依旧笼罩在你的身上？

哈：不，陛下；我已经在太阳里晒得太久了。

这里，主要困难在于莎士比亚让哈姆莱特使用了 kin 和 kind 以及 son 和 sun 两组双关语。kind 一词又有双关意义，翻译无法完全表达，只能各译一个侧面。结果，梁和卞两先生还得用注释补足其义，朱译则连注释也没有。这种地方，能读原文注释本的人才能充分领略莎氏原意。

哈姆莱特在旁白里说：比亲戚多一点——本来我是你的侄子，现在又成了你的儿子，确实不是一般的亲戚关系啊；然而却比 kind 少一点——kind 有两层意思，一是"同类相求"的亲近感，一是"与人为善"的善意感，我同你没有共同语言，我也不知道你是安的什么心。这话只能对自己说，在舞台上假定对方是听不到的。哈姆莱特的第二句话是公开的俏皮话：哪里有什么阴云呀，我在太阳里晒得不行呢。sun 是跟 clouds 相对；太阳又意味着国王的恩宠，"你对我太好了，我怎么会阴郁呢？"sun 又跟 son 谐音，"做你的儿子，我领教得够了。"原文并不是像梁实秋所说的那样晦涩难解。可是含义太复杂，有隐藏的深层感情，所以无法译得完全。

（二）语法。有些现象，按现代英语语法的标准看，似乎是错误的，但在当时并不错，是属于中世纪英语的残余因素。例如有些动词过去分词的词尾变化、代词的所有格形式、主谓语数的不一致、关系代词和介词的用法等方面，都有一些和现在不同的情况。注释里说明了，可以举一反三去理解。

（三）词序的颠倒和穿插。词尾屈折变化较多的中世纪英语本来对词序没有严格的要求。伊丽莎白时代继承了这种习惯。同时，诗的节律和押韵要求对词序作一定的灵活处理。莎士比亚的舞台语言以鲜明、有力、生动为首要考虑，有时他就把语法和句法放在从属的地位。在激动的台词中，由于思路、感情的变化，语言也常有脱出常规的变化。这些地方，有了注释的指点，理解就容易得多。

（四）典故。莎士比亚用典很多。古希腊、罗马神话，《圣经》故事，英国民间传说，历史逸事……他都随手拈来。其中有一大部分对于英美读者来说乃是常识，但中国读者就很需要注释的帮助。

（五）文化背景。注释可以提供关于基督教义、中世纪传统观点、文艺复兴时期新的主张、英国习俗等方面的知识。

除上述以外，还有莎剧中影射时事，以及版本考据诸问题，在注释本中可以详细论述，也可以简单提及。

世界文豪莫不是语言大师，而要真正理解和欣赏一位大师的文笔，当然非读他的原著不成。出版莎士比亚注释本，首先是为了让中国读者便于买到和读到他的原著。不过我们自知现出的几十种在版本、注释和其他方面还存在不足之处，希望读者多提意见，以便今后不断改进。

裘克安

前 言

威廉·莎士比亚于1564年4月出生于英国中部埃文河畔斯特拉福镇上一个相当富裕的市民家里。他在镇上的文法学校念过书，主要读拉丁文，可能也读点希腊文。离开学校后，他曾帮助他父亲做过各种手艺和生意，据说还当过乡间学校的助理教师。大约在1585年他到了伦敦，在剧院里干些下等工作，后来当过演员并开始了戏剧创作活动，起初改编别人的老剧本，然后转到独立创作。现在保存下来的38部剧本（一说37部），只不过是他在伦敦时期所写的剧本中的一部分。大约在1612年，他离开伦敦回到斯特拉福镇；1616年4月逝世，享年52岁。

莎士比亚是一个伟大的戏剧创作大师，同时又是一个完全掌握了诗的语言的天才诗人。马克思称道过："莎士比亚的创作是世界艺术顶峰之一。"

《威尼斯商人》为莎士比亚四大喜剧之一，内容丰富多彩。从剧情的发展看，正当安东尼奥在法庭上面临悲剧，生命危在旦夕之际，鲍西娅以她卓越的机智和聪明，发表了服人以理、动人以情的辩词，将放高利贷的犹太人夏洛克击败，使悲剧转变为喜剧。从剧本的结构看，莎士比亚像在其他很多剧本中一样，充分利用了平行结构(parallelism)。该剧本包含两个主要线索："挑选彩盒"与"借债割肉"，用鲍西娅在这两个故事中的主导作用将它们巧妙地连接起来。巴萨尼奥是威尼斯一位身无分文的贵族青年，为了向品貌双全的富家嗣女鲍西娅求婚，到他的好友安东尼奥那里借钱；而安东尼奥因货船尚未到港，只好向经常被他侮辱的犹太高利贷者夏洛克借款，被迫立下一张契约，如不按时偿还，就让夏洛克在他身上割一磅肉。巴萨尼奥和鲍西娅一见钟情，彼此相爱。但鲍西娅的父亲在遗嘱中规定，求婚者必须在三个彩盒中挑中装有鲍西娅小像的彩盒才能得到她。当巴萨尼奥选中后，他和鲍西娅正在情投意合地互相倾诉爱慕时，巴萨尼奥的朋友葛莱西安诺和鲍西娅的侍女尼莉莎也偷偷地在一边谈情说爱，互相交心，刚好配成两对。他们正高兴时，传来消息，安东尼奥的货船遇难，债务到期他将被罚割一磅肉。聪明的鲍西娅毅然扮作律师，携带着扮作她的书记的尼莉莎，去威尼斯营救安东尼奥。在法庭上的辩论中，鲍西娅以惊人的才智和非凡的风度，驳倒了居心报复的夏洛克，赢了这宗棘手的官司。鲍西娅的智慧、美丽、温柔、淘气，在读者与观众的脑海中形成了一个完美的女性形象。而反角夏洛克虽然爱财如命，在勒索一磅肉时他欲置安东尼奥于死地，但莎士比亚却借他的口，对资产阶级进行了控诉，他们满口仁义道德，实质上对劳动人民压迫剥削无所不用其极。同时莎士比亚用夏洛克对民族和宗教歧视的抨击和对妻子和女儿的感情，把他的形象描绘得生动复杂，有血有肉，而不只是简单地代表抽象的性格——贪婪和残酷。

《威尼斯商人》中的语言是多样化的，虽然主要是无韵诗，但掺杂了很多散文成分，有诗歌、有法庭演说、有独白、有机智的评论（如鲍西娅在对几个求婚者的评论中，非常幽默地讽刺了当时欧洲一些国家的时尚；巴萨尼奥在选盒子时的独白中也揭露了宗教的伪善和美貌的虚幻等）。第五幕第一场罗兰佐和杰西卡在月夜交谈中的每一段话都用“in such a night”开始，引证了古典文学中一些充满浪漫色彩的爱情故事，富有诗情画意，这同前面法庭审判的严肃气氛形成鲜明对照，巧妙地体现了生活中悲与喜、严肃气氛与浪漫情调互相交错的多样性和复杂性。

《威尼斯商人》约写于 1596 年。16 世纪 90 年代初马洛的《马耳他犹太人》上演，颇有名气。1594 年 6 月 7 日犹太医生洛佩斯以阴谋毒害女王罪被处死。莎士比亚就是在伦敦群众对犹太问题很有兴趣的气氛中写出这个剧本的。但莎士比亚无意影射时政，而是利用一些旧有故事材料进行再创作，并就金钱、利息、友谊、爱情、法律、慈悲等问题提出自己的看法，因而本剧也有一定的象征意义。《威尼斯商人》于 1598 年 7 月 22 日在书业公所进行登记,1600 年出版第一个四开本,1609 年出版第二个四开本,1623 年收入对开的剧作全集。三个版本没有重大的差别。这里印出的基本上是 1965 年纽约埃尔蒙特(Airmont)莎士比亚经典丛书的版本,但对第二幕的分场等作了一些变动。

为了帮助读者阅读和欣赏这一名著,按行码的顺序作了比较详细的注释。除释义外,对某些语法修辞特点也作了说明。注释承裘克安同志细心审校修改,特此表示衷心的感谢。

张文庭

1988 年 12 月于湖南师大

THE MERCHANT OF VENICE

DRAMATIS PERSONAE

DUKE OF VENICE.

PRINCE OF MOROCCO, } *suitors to Portia.*
PRINCE OF ARRAGON, }

ANTONIO, *a merchant of Venice.*

BASSANIO, *his kinsman and friend.*

SOLANIO, }
SALARINO, } *friends to Antonio and Bassanio.*
GRATIANO, }

LORENZO, *in love with Jessica.*

SHYLOCK, *a rich Jew.*

TUBAL, *a Jew, his friend.*

LAUNCELOT GOBBO, *a clown, servant to Shylock.*

OLD GOBBO, *father to Launcelot.*

LEONARDO, *servant to Bassanio.*

BALTHAZAR, } *servants to Portia.*
STEPHANO, }

PORTIA, *a rich heiress.*

NERISSA, *her waiting-maid.*

JESSICA, *daughter to Shylock.*

MAGNIFICOES OF VENICE, OFFICERS OF THE COURT OF JUSTICE, GAOLER, SERVANTS, *and other* ATTENDANTS.

SCENE— *Partly at Venice, and partly at Belmont, the seat of Portia, on the Continent.*

注　　释

Dramatis personae[拉丁语:ˈdrɑːmətis pəːˈsəunai]:剧中人物

Arragon[ˈærəgən]:阿拉贡(西班牙省名)

Antonio[ænˈtəuniəu]:安东尼奥

Bassanio[bəˈsɑːniəu]:巴萨尼奥

Solanio[səuˈleiniəu]

Salarino[ˌsæləˈrinəu]

Gratiano[ˌgrɑːʃiˈɑːnəu]

Lorenzo[lɔˈrenzəu]:罗兰佐

Shylock[ˈʃɑːˈlɔk]:夏洛克

Tubal[ˈtjuːbəl]

Launcelot Gobbo[ˈlɑːnslət ˈgɔbəu]

Leonardo[ˌli(ː)əˈnɑːdəu]

Balthazar[ˌbælθəˈzɑː]

Stephano[ˈstefənəu]

Portia[ˈpɔːʃiə]:鲍西娅

Nerissa[niˈrisə]:尼莉莎

Jessica[ˈdʒesikə]

Magnificoes[mægˈnifikəuz]〈意大利语〉:士绅

Belmont[ˈbelmɔnt]:贝尔蒙特(鲍西娅邸宅所在地,在大陆上,而威尼斯城则在岛上)

ACT I

SCENE I

Venice. A street.

Enter ANTONIO, SALARINO, *and* SOLANIO.

ANTONIO.
In sooth I know not why I am so sad:
It wearies me; you say it wearies you;
But how I caught it, found it, or came by it,
What stuff 'tis made of, whereof it is born,
I am to learn;
And such a want-wit sadness makes of me,
That I have much ado to know myself.

SALARINO.
Your mind is tossing on the ocean;
There, where your argosies with portly sail, —
Like signiors and rich burghers of the flood,
Or, as it were, the pageants of the sea, —
Do overpeer the petty traffickers,
That curtsey to them, do them reverence,
As they fly by them with their woven wings.

SOLANIO.
Believe me, sir, had I such venture forth,
The better part of my affections would
Be with my hopes abroad. I should be still
Plucking the grass, to know where sits the wind;
Peering in maps for ports, and piers, and road;
And every object that might make me fear
Misfortune to my ventures, out of doubt
Would make me sad.

SALARINO.

I.i （第一幕第一场，后类推）（以下黑体数字为行码）

* 无韵诗是没有脚韵的诗，每行十个音节，大体分为五个抑扬格（轻重音）的音步，如本剧开始的两行可以分析如下：

In soóth |I knów|nót why| I ám | so sád：

It wéa|ries mé；|you sáy|it wéa|ries yóu；

1 **In sooth**：in truth, in fact.

3 **came by**：got.

4 **stuff**：material. **whereof**：of what.

5 **am to learn**：am yet to learn；have not yet learned.

6 **want-wit**：（动词加宾语构成的复合词）person wanting wit；fool；idiot. **Such…me**：Sadness makes such a fool of me.

7 **ado**：difficulty；trouble. **know myself**：相当于当时流行的拉丁文格言 nosce te ipsum，意思是神志清醒，有自知之明。

9 **argosies**：great merchant ships. **portly**：majestic.

10 **signiors**（现在拼法为 signor）［意大利语，ˈsiːnjɔː］：先生。**burghers**［ˈbəːgəz］：citizens, businessmen. **flood**：sea.

11 **as it were**（插入句）：宛如。 **pageants**［ˈpædʒənts］：shows, spectacles, wheeled stages of Miracle Plays，奇迹戏的彩车。

12 **overpeer**：look down on. **petty traffickers**：小商人。

13 **curtsey**：行屈膝礼。 **do them reverence**：bow to them.

14 **woven wings**：sails.

15 **venture**：a thing put to rish，冒风险之物（这里指船队）。**forth**：off, away from home.

16 **better**：greater.

17 **still**：always，constantly.

18 **sits**：blows (from a particular quarter).（英谚）A straw shows which way the wind blows.

19 **roads**：roadsteads, anchorages，停泊处。

22 **Would make**：主语为 object.

My wind, cooling my broth.
Would blow me to an ague when I thought
What harm a wind too great might do at sea.
I should not see the sandy hour-glass run,
But I should think of shallows and of flats;
And see my wealthy Andrew dockt in sand,
Vailing her high-top lower than her ribs,
To kiss her burial. Should I go to church,
And see the holy edifice of stone,
And not bethink me straight of dangerous rocks,
Which touching but my gentle vessel's side,
Would scatter all her spices on the stream;
Enrobe the roaring waters with my silks;
And, in a word, but even now worth this,
And now worth nothing? Shall I have the thought
To think on this; and shall I lack the thought,
That such a thing bechanced would make me sad?
But tell not me; I know Antonio
Is sad to think upon his merchandise.

ANTONIO.

Believe me, no: I thank my fortune for it,
My ventures are not in one bottom trusted,
Nor to one place; nor is my whole estate
Upon the fortune of this present year:
Therefore my merchandise makes me not sad.

SOLANIO.

Why, then you are in love.

ANTONIO.

Fie, fie!

SALARINO.

Not in love neither? Then let's say you're sad,
Because you are not merry: and 'twere as easy
For you to laugh, and leap, and say you are merry,
Because you are not sad. Now, by two-headed Janus,

22 **wind**: breath.

23 **ague** ['eigju:]:寒战。

25—26 **I should not…/But I should think…**: I would not … without thinking…. **sandy hour-glass**: 沙漏计时器。

26 **shallows and flats**: sandbanks and shoals,浅滩和沙洲。

27 **Andrew**: 1596 年一艘有名的西班牙船的名字。 **dockt**: doked; placed as in a dry dock; run aground,搁浅。

28 **Vailing**: lowering or bowing as in surrender,低头,俯首。 **high-top**: masthead,桅顶。 **ribs**: 船的肋材。

29 **burial**: burial-place.

31 **bethink me**: think.

33 **spices**: 香料。当时欧洲船只到东、西印度群岛廉价购买香料,回欧洲后可赚大钱。香料主要用于腌肉和制香肠时调味。

35—36 **but…nothing**: just now worth so much and at the next moment worth nothing.

37 **on**: of.

38 **bechanced**: as happened.

42 **bottom**: 船舱(这里指船)。系用部分指全体的提喻(synecdoche). **trusted**: consigned.

43 **estate**: property.

44 **Upon**: dependent upon,取决于。

46 **Fie**! (an exclamation of contempt or dislike):呸!去你的!

47 **Not…neither?**: not…either (莎士比亚时代常用双重否定 double negatives 表示否定)。

48 **'twere**: it would be (当时主句中的虚拟语气常不用 would 或 should).

50 **by…**: (赌咒语) I swear by…. **Janus** ['dʒeinəs]: Roman god (the porter of Heaven) with two faces, one in front and one behind,两面门神。

Nature hath framed strange fellows in her time:
Some that will evermore peep through their eyes,
And laugh, like parrots, at a bag-piper;
And other of such vinegar aspect,
That they'll not show their teeth in way of smile,
Though Nestor swear that jest be laughable.

SOLANIO.

Here comes Bassanio, your most noble kinsman,
Gratiano, and Lorenzo. Fare ye well:
We leave you now with better company.

SALARINO.

I would have stay'd till I had made you merry,
If worthier friends had not prevented me.

ANTONIO.

Your worth is very dear in my regard.
I take it, your own business calls on you,
And you embrace th' occasion to depart.

Enter BASSANIO, LORENZO, *and* GRATIANO.

SALARINO.

Good morrow, my good lords.

BASSANIO.

Good signiors both, when shall we laugh? say, when?
You grow exceeding strange: must it be so?

SALARINO.

We'll make our leisures to attend on yours.

[*Exeunt* SALARINO *and* SOLANIO.

LORENZO.

My Lord Bassanio, since you have found Antonio,
We two will leave you: but, at dinner-time,
I pray you, have in mind where we must meet.

BASSANIO.

51 **framed**：made. **in her time**：当初，过去。**Nature**：被视为是女性。

52 **evermore**：always.

53 **laugh…bag-piper**：像鹦鹉听到风笛时的无端发笑（苏格兰风笛的音乐是哀婉的，对之发笑完全没来由）。

54 **other**：others（这种用法常见）。 **vinegar aspect**：sour appearance.

55 **in way of smile**：in the manner of a smile（介词短语中常省略冠词）。

56 **Nestor**：希腊传说中最老、最有智慧的首领。

58 **ye**：you.

61 **worthier**：更高贵的。 **prevented**：anticipated，forestalled（他们已经来到，我不必这样做了）。

62 **worth**：valuable quality，worthiness，高贵的人品。 **dear**：precious（接上句的 worthier 而言）。 **regard**：estimation.

63 **take it**：think，suppose. **calls on**：makes a claim on.

64 **embrace**：take. **occasion**：chance.

65 **Good morrow**：good morning.

66 **when…laugh?**：何时我们可以欢聚一下？

67 **exceeding**：very. **strange**：cold，distant.

68 **We'll…yours**：We'll make ourselves available when you are free. **leisures**：leisure moments. **to attend**：现在用法，这个不定式的 to 应省略。

Exeunt ［拉丁语，'eksiʌnt］：go out（为 exit 的复数）。

71 **have in mind**：remember.

I will not fail you.

GRATIANO.

You look not well, Signior Antonio:
You have too much respect upon the world:
They lose it that do buy it with much care:
Believe me, you are marvellously changed.

ANTONIO.

I hold the world but as the world, Gratiano;
A stage, where every man must play a part,
And mine a sad one.

GRATIANO.

Let me play the fool:
With mirth and laughter let old wrinkles come;
And let my liver rather heat with wine
Than my heart cool with mortifying groans.
Why should a man, whose blood is warm within,
Sit like his grandsire cut in alabaster?
Sleep when he wakes? and creep into the jaundice
By being peevish? I tell thee what, Antonio,—
I love thee, and it is my love that speaks,—
There are a sort of men, whose visages
Do cream and mantle like a standing pond;
And do a wilful stillness entertain,
With purpose to be drest in an opinion
Of wisdom, gravity, profound conceit;
As who should say, 'I am Sir Oracle
And when I ope my lips, let no dog bark!'
O my Antonio, I do know of these,
That therefore only are reputed wise
For saying nothing; when, I am very sure,
If they should speak, would almost damn those ears,
Which, hearing them, would call their brothers fools.
I'll tell thee more of this another time:
But fish not, with this melancholy bait,

74 have respect upon：look with respect upon，have regard for. **the world**：worldly matters.

75 it：代 world. **care**：忧虑。

76 marvellously：greatly.

77 hold：regard，look upon. **but**：only.

79 fool：丑角。

82 mortifying：deadly，killing，致命的。 **mortifying groans**：讨命的呻吟（sighs were supposed to consume the heart's bllod，and so to be deadly）.

84 Sit…grandsire：sit still and solemn，like a figure of his grandfather on a tombstone. **alabaster**：雪花石膏（英国教堂中常用雪花石膏做墓碑）。

85 jaundice：disorder in the bile（胆汁），caused by，and causing，intense depression，黄疸病（因忧郁而生此病并引起忧郁）。

88 visages：faces.

89 cream and mantle：become covered with a pale thick scum. **standing**：stagnant.

90 entertain：maintain.

91 With…opinion：in order to get a reputation.

92 conceit：thought.

93 As who：As any one who. **Sir Oracle**：the wise one who knows everything，说话像神谕般的人。

94 ope：open.

98—99 would：they would. **ears**：listeners（为提喻 Synecdoche）. **If…fools**：If they should say anything，their words would make their listeners call them fools and be damned for doing so.（见《圣经・新约・马太福音》第 5 章 22 节，“凡骂弟兄是笨蛋的，难免地狱的火”。）

101 fish…bait：don't put on this serious and melancholy air as a bait，别拿忧郁做钓饵。

For this fool-gudgeon, this opinion.—
Come, good Lorenzo.—Fare ye well awhile:
I'll end my exhortation after dinner.

LORENZO.

Well, we will leave you, then, till dinner-time:
I must be one of these same dumb wise men,
For Gratiano never lets me speak.

GRATIANO.

Well, keep me company but two years moe,
Thou shalt not know the sound of thine own tongue.

ANTONIO.

Farewell: I'll grow a talker for this gear.

GRATIANO.

Thanks, i'faith, for silence is only commendable
In a neat's tongue dried, and a maid not vendible.

[*Exeunt* GRATIANO *and* LORENZO.

ANTONIO.

Is that any thing now?

BASSANIO.

Gratiano speaks an infinite deal of nothing, more than any man in all Venice. His reasons are as two grains of wheat hid in two bushels of chaff: you shall seek all day ere you find them; and when you have them, they are not worth the search.

ANTONIO.

Well; tell me now, what lady is the same
To whom you swore a secret pilgrimage,
That you to-day promised to tell me of?

BASSANIO.

'Tis not unknown to you, Antonio,
How much I have disabled mine estate.
By something showing a more swelling port
Than my faint means would grant continuance:
Nor do I now make moan to be abridged

102 **gudgeon** [ˈgʌdʒən]：a small fish easily caught. **this opinion**：this reputation of wisdom 等，见上 91—92 行。

104 **exhortation**：敦劝。

108 **but**：only. **moe**：more.

110 **grow**：become. **gear**：chatter，stuff(i.e. What you have said against silent people).

111 **commendable** [kəˈmendəbl]：praiseworthy.

112 **neat's tongue**：ox tongue. **vendible**：saleable，marriageable.

113 **Is…now?**：Now，do his words make any sense?

115 **reasons**：arguments，intelligent remarks.

117 **ere**：before.

120 **pilgrimage**：long journey，中世纪常把对情人的追求比作朝圣的旅途。

123 **disabled mine estate**：reduced my fortune.

124 **something** (adv.)：somewhat. **swelling port**：extravagant way of living.

125 **faint**：poor. **grant**：permit.

126 **make moan**：moan(当时 make 常和名词构成短语，以代替动词，如 make reply，make answer 等)。 **to be abridged**：about being debarred.

From such a noble rate; but my chief care
Is, to come fairly off from the great debts,
Wherein my time, something too prodigal,
Hath left me gaged. To you, Antonio,
I owe the most, in money and in love;
And from your love I have a warranty
To unburden all my plots and purposes
How to get clear of all the debts I owe.

ANTONIO.

I pray you, good Bassanio, let me know it;
And if it stand, as you yourself still do,
Within the eye of honour, be assured
My purse, my person, my extremest means,
Lie all unlockt to your occasions.

BASSANIO.

In my school-days, when I had lost one shaft,
I shot his fellow of the selfsame flight
The selfsame way with more advised watch,
To find the other forth; and by advent'ring both,
I oft found both: I urge this childhood proof,
Because what follows is pure innocence.
I owe you much; and, like a wilful youth,
That which I owe is lost: but if you please
To shoot another arrow that self way
Which you did shoot the first, I do not doubt,
As I will watch the aim, or to find both,
Or bring your latter hazard back again,
And thankfully rest debtor for the first.

ANTONIO.

You know me well; and herein spend but time
To wind about my love with circumstance;
And out of doubt you do me now more wrong
In making question of my uttermost,
Than if you had made waste of all I have:

127 **noble rate**: splendid style of living.

128 **come … off from**: get rid of, pay off. **fairly**: properly, honorably.

129 **time**: way of life. **prodigal**: extravagant.

130 **Hath**: has 在中世纪和诗体英语中,第三人称单数动词有时用(e)th 结尾。 **gaged** [geidʒd]: engaged, bound.

132 **warranty**: authorization, permission.

133 **unburden**: disclose. **plots**: plans(无贬义)。

136 **still**: always.

137 **Within…honor**: within the scope of honor's vision.

138 **my person**: myself. **extremest**: utmost.

139 **occasions**: needs,需求。

140 **shaft**: arrow.

141 **his**: its 是中世纪英语 it 的所有格。 **his fellow**: its fellow, another similar arrow. **selfsame**: same. **of the selfsame fight**: (箭术上的用语)轻重、长短、射程相等的。

142 **way**: direction. **advised watch**: careful attention.

143 **forth**: out. **advent'ring**: adventuring, risking.

144 **oft**: often. **urge**: put forward in argument. **childhood proof**: childhood's proof (experience).

145 **pure innocence**: naïveté, folly. **what…innocence**: 我接着要讲的是一个纯真的幼稚想法。

146 **wilful**: 任性的,固执的。

147 **if you please**: if it pleases you.

148 **self**: same.

150 **As**: so. **or**: either.

151 **hazard**: risk, speculation,冒险之物,投机之物。

152 **rest**: remain.

153 **spend but time**: only waste time.

154 **To wind about**: in circling around. **circumstance**: circumlocution.

155 **out of**: without.

156 **making question of**: questioning. **my uttermost**: my doing my utmost.

157 **made waste of**: wasted.

Then do but say to me what I should do,
That in your knowledge may by me be done,
And I am prest unto it: therefore, speak.

BASSANIO.

In Belmont is a lady richly left;
And she is fair, and, fairer than that word,
Of wondrous virtues: sometimes from her eyes
I did receive fair speechless messages:
Her name is Portia; noting undervalued
To Cato's daughter, Brutus' Portia:
Nor is the wide world ignorant of her worth;
For the four winds blow in from every coast
Renowned suitors: and her sunny locks
Hang on her temples like a golden fleece;
Which makes her seat of Belmont Colchos' strond,
And many Jasons come in quest of her.
O my Antonio, had I but the means
To hold a rival place with one of them,
I have a mind presages me such thrift,
That I should questionless be fortunate!

ANTONIO.

Thou know'st that all my fortunes are at sea;
Neither have I money, nor commodity
To raise a present sum: therefore, go forth;
Try what my credit can in Venice do:
That shall be rackt, even to the uttermost,
To furnish thee to Belmont, to fair Portia.
Go, presently inquire, and so will I,
Where money is; and I no question make,
To have it of my trust, or for my sake. [*Exeunt*.

158 **but**：only.

160 **prest**：ready. **unto it**：to do it.

161 **richly left**：left with a rich legacy，有巨额遗产。

162 **fair**：白皮肤，浅金色头发，当时认为是最美的。

163 **wondrous**：wonderful. **sometimes**：formerly.

165 **nothing undervalued**：not in the least inferior.

166 **To**：by the side of，in comparison with. **Cato** ['keitəu]：古罗马哲学家（95—46 B.C.），其女也叫 Portia，是罗马政治家 Brutus ['bru:təs]之妻。

169 **Renowned suitors**：有名的求婚者。

170—172 希腊传说中，英雄 Jason['dʒeisn]航海到 Colchos ['kɔlkɔs]，得到该地公主女巫 Medea[mi'diə]的帮助，经历艰险，取得金羊毛并带回 Medea 做妻子。 **seat**：宅邸所在地。 **strond**：strand，sea-shore.

172 **in quest of her**：to ask her hand，向她求婚。

175 **mind presages**：feeling that foretells（that 省略）。 **thrift**：success，profit.

176 **questionless** (adv.)：undoubtedly.

177 **fortunes**：property，riches.

178 **commodity**：货品（这里指作为抵押品的货物）。

179 **raise…sum**：筹措一笔现款。 **present**：immediate.

180 **credit**：信用。

181 **rackt**：stretched as upon a rack，extended.

182 **furnish**：equip，supply with what is necessary.

183 **presently**：at once.

184 **no question make**：have no objection，agree.

185 **of**：on.

SCENE II

Belmont. A room in PORTIA'S *house.*

Enter PORTIA *and* NERISSA.

PORTIA.

By my troth, Nerissa, my little body is aweary of this great world.

NERISSA.

You would be, sweet madam, if your miseries were in the same abundance as your good fortunes are: and yet, for aught I see, they are as sick that surfeit with too much, as they that starve with nothing. It is no mean happiness, therefore, to be seated in the mean: superfluity comes sooner by white hairs; but competency lives longer.

PORTIA.

Good sentences, and well pronounced.

NERISSA.

They would be better, if well follow'd.

PORTIA.

If to do were as easy as to know what were good to do, chapels had been churches, and poor men's cottages princes' palaces. It is a good divine that follows his own instructions: I can easier teach twenty what were good to be done, than be one of the twenty to follow mine own teaching. The brain may devise laws for the blood; but a hot temper leaps o'er a cold decree: such a hare is madness the youth, to skip o'er the meshes of good-counsel the cripple. But this reasoning is not in the fashion to choose me a husband: — O me, the word 'choose'! I may neither choose who I would, nor refuse who I dislike;

I.ii

1 troth：truth，faith. **Nerissa**：此名有“黑发女郎”之义。 **By my troth**：确实（口语中的强调用语，其前省略了“I swear”）. **aweary**：weary.

3 You：Nerissa 不是佣仆而是有地位的侍女，故她称 Portia 为 you，而不称 thou.

5 for aught I see：for anything I know，as far as I know. **they are as sick that…**：those people are as sick who…. **surfeit**：be overfed.

7—8 mean：small. **be seated in the mean**：be in the middle of two extremes，have neither too much nor too little. **superfluity**：excess.

8—9 comes … by：acquires，causes. **competency**：moderation，modest means.

10 sentences：sententiae，maxims.

13 chapels had been churches：small churches would have become big ones. chapel 是教堂内一角祈祷处，或附属性小教堂。

14 divine：preacher，clergyman.

17 brain：reason，mind，理智，头脑。

18 blood：passions，impulses，感情，冲动。

19 leap（skip）**o'er**：ingnore，overlook. **madness**：狂热，和 youth 同位。

20 meshes：net. **good-counsel**：好的忠告，和 cripple 同位。**meshes**：捉野兔时张的网。

21 reasoning：arguing，发议论。 **fashion**：manner，way，方式。

22 O me：（表感叹）Oh，dear me.

so is the will of a living daughter curb'd by the will of a dead father. — Is it not hard, Nerissa, that I cannot choose one, nor refuse none?

NERISSA.

Your father was ever virtuous; and holy men, at their death, have good inspirations: therefore, the lottery, that he hath devised in these three chests of gold, silver, and lead, — whereof who chooses his meaning chooses you, —will, no doubt, never be chosen by any rightly, but one who shall rightly love. But what warmth is there in your affection towards any of these princely suitors that are already come?

PORTIA.

I pray thee, over-name them; and as thou namest them, I will describe them; and, according to my description, level at my affection.

NERISSA.

First, there is the Neapolitan prince.

PORTIA.

Ay, that's a colt indeed, for he doth nothing but talk of his horse; and he makes it a great appropriation to his own good parts, that he can shoe him himself. I am much afeard my lady his mother play'd false with a smith.

NERISSA.

Then there is the County Palatine.

PORTIA.

He doth nothing but frown; as who should say, 'An you will not have me, choose:' he hears merry tales, and smiles not: I fear he will prove the weeping philosopher when he grows old, being so full of unmannerly sadness in his youth. I had rather be married to a Death's-head with a bone in his mouth

24—25 will…will：前一个指“意愿”，后一个指“遗嘱”。

26 nor refuse none：nor refuse one（双否定仍表否定）。

28 inspirations：sudden thoughts，ideas.

29 lottery：lucky draw，抽彩签。 **chests**：caskets（见下）。

30—31 chooses his meaning：chooses what your father meant to be chosen.

32 but：except.

34—35 are-already/come：have come 当时对 verbs of motion 常有这种用法。

36 over-name：enumerate，repeat the names of.

38 level：aim，guess. **level at my affection**：guess my feelings towards them.

39 Neapolitan [niəˈpɔlitən]：意大利那不勒斯的。

40 colt：小马驹（转意不更事的青年）。

41—42 appropriation：attribution，asset. **parts**：gifts，天赋，才能。 **him**：it.

43 afeard：afraid.

44 play'd false with：had an affair with…，与……私通。

45 County：Count. **Palatine** [ˈpælətain]：旧时德国莱茵河西岸地区。

46 as who should say：as (like) one who should say. **An**：if.

47 choose：do what you please.

48—49 weeping philosopher：the Greek philosopher Heraclitus [hiˈræklitəs，about 540—475B.C.]：who wept over the follies of mankind.

50 unmanneriy (adj.)：uncivil，indecent，不得体的。

51 Death's-head：象征死亡的骷髅和两根交叉的骨头。

than to either of these: — God defend me from these two!

NERISSA.

How say you by the French lord, Monsieur Le Bon?

PORTIA.

God made him, and therefore let him pass for a man. In truth, I know it is a sin to be a mocker: but, he! — why, he hath a horse better than the Neapolitan's; a better bad habit of frowning than the Count Palatine : he is every man in no man; if a throstle sing, he falls straight a-capering; he will fence with his own shadow: if I should marry him, I should marry twenty husbands. If he would despise me, I would forgive him; for if he love me to madness, I shall never requite him.

NERISSA.

What say you, then, to Falconbridge, the young baron of England?

PORTIA.

You know I say nothing to him: for he understands not me, nor I him: he hath neither Latin, French, nor Italian; and you will come into the court and swear that I have a poor pennyworth in the English. He is a proper man's picture; but, alas, who can converse with a dumb-show? How oddly he is suited! I think he bought his doublet in Italy, his round hose in France, his bonnet in Germany, and his behaviour every where.

NERISSA.

What think you of the Scottish lord, his neighbour?

PORTIA.

That he hath a neighbourly charity in him; for he borrow'd a box of the ear of the Englishman, and swore he would pay him again when he was able:

54 How say you by：what do you say about，what do you think of. **Monsieur**［法语，mə'sjəː］：先生。 **Le Bon**［法语，lə bɔn］：好。

55 pass for：充当。

59 every man in no man：one of changeable nature，without his own personality.

60 throstle：thrust，鸫，画眉。 **falls…a-capering**：falls to dancing，begins to cut capers. a-是从古英语 on 演变而来。 **straight**：at once.

64 requite：repay.

68 hath：knows.

70 a poor pennyworth：very little.

71 proper：handsome. **a proper man's picture**：外表看起来挺漂亮。

72 dumb-show：pantomime，哑剧(转义木偶)。

73—74 doublet：coat. **round hose**：short breeches，短灯笼裤。 **bonnet**：软帽。

67—75 You…every where：这是当时对英国人常有的批评，说他们只会讲英语，不会讲别种语言，穿着却五花八门地模仿别国式样。Poria 对其他几国来的求婚者的评论，也具有一般性。

77 That：I think that. **neighbourly**：friendly，kind. **charity**：慈善(常被嘲笑地用来指怯懦)。

78 borrow'd a box of the ear of：receive a blow from.

I think the Frenchman became his surety, and seal'd under for another.

NERISSA.

How like you the young German, the Duke of Saxony's nephew?

PORTIA.

Very vilely in the morning, when he is sober; and most vilely in the afternoon, when he is drunk: when he is best, he is a little worse than a man; and when he is worst, he is little better than a beast. An the worst fall that ever fell, I hope I shall make shift to go without him.

NERISSA.

If he should offer to choose, and choose the right casket, you should refuse to perform your father's will, if you should refuse to accept him.

PORTIA.

Therefore, for fear of the worst, I pray thee, set a deep glass of Rhenish wine on the contrary casket; for, if the devil be within, and that temptation without, I know he will choose it. I will do anything, Nerissa, ere I will be married to a sponge.

NERISSA.

You need not fear, lady, the having any of these lords: they have acquainted me with their determinations; which is, indeed, to return to their home, and to trouble you with no more suit, unless you may be won by some other sort than your father's imposition, depending on the caskets.

PORTIA.

If I live to be as old as Sibylla, I will die as chaste as Diana, unless I be obtain'd by the manner of my father's will. I am glad this parcel of wooers are so reasonable; for there is not one among them but I

80—81 seal'd under：put his seal under the Scot's on the bond. **another**：another box of the ear in addition to the one to be repaid.

82 Saxony [ˈsæksni]：旧时德国东部一地区(今莱比锡以南)。

85 vilely：bad.

89—90 An：if. **fall**：happen，befall. **An the worst fall**：如果碰上最坏的运气。 **make shift**：manage，设法。 **go without him**：摆脱他(不嫁给他)。

92 (第一个)**you should**：you would.

95 Rhenish wine：莱茵河流域产的白葡萄酒。 **contrary**：opposite.

96 if：even if. **that temptation**：指酒。

98 ere：before. **sponge**：drunkard.

99 the having：动名词前有时用定冠词。

103 by some other sort：in some other manner.

104 imposition：injunction，order.

105 Sibylla [ˈsibilə]：希腊神话中年老的女预言家。

106 Diana [daiˈænə]：希腊神话中的月亮女神，象征贞洁。

107 parcel：small party.

108 but I：that I do not.

dote on his very absence; and I pray God grant them a fair departure.

NERISSA.

Do you not remember, lady, in your father's time, a Venetian, a scholar and a soldier, that came hither in company of the Marquis of Montferrat?

PORTIA.

Yes, yes, it was Bassanio: as I think, so was he call'd.

NERISSA.

True, madam: he, of all the men that ever my foolish eyes lookt upon, was the best deserving a fair lady.

PORTIA.

I remember him well; and I remember him worthy of thy praise.

Enter a SERVANT.

How now! what news?

SERVANT.

The four strangers seek for you, madam, to take their leave: and there is a forerunner come from a fifth, the Prince of Morocco; who brings word, the prince his master will be here to-night.

PORTIA.

If I could bid the fifth welcome with so good a heart as I can bid the other four farewell, I should be glad of his approach: if he have the condition of a saint and the complexion of a devil, I had rather he should shrive me than wive me.
Come, Nerissa.—Sirrah, go before.—
Whiles we shut the gates upon one wooer, another knocks at the door. [*Exeunt.*

109 **dote on**：love.

112 **Venetian** [və'niːʃən]：威尼斯人。

113 **Marquis** ['mɑːkwis]：侯爵。 **Montferrat** [mɔnt'feræt]：Montferrato 是意大利北部一大家族。

127 **condition**：quality，character.

128 **complexion**：appearance. **complexion of a devil**：the devil was painted black.

129 **shrive**：hear a person's confession and give him absolution，听忏悔并赦罪。 **wive**：以……为妻。

130 **Sirrah** ['sirə]：(form of address to an inferior) 对下属打招呼的用语。

131 **Whiles**：while.

SCENE III

Venice. A public place.

Enter BASSANIO *with* SHYLOCK *the Jew.*

SHYLOCK.

Three thousand ducats, —well.

BASSANIO.

Ay, sir, for three months.

SHYLOCK.

For three months,—well.

BASSANIO.

For the which, as I told you, Antonio shall be bound.

SHYLOCK.

Antonio shall become bound,—well.

BASSANIO.

May you stead me? will you pleasure me? shall I know your answer?

SHYLOCK.

Three thousand ducats for three months, and Antonio bound.

BASSANIO.

Your answer to that.

SHYLOCK.

Antonio is a good man.

BASSANIO.

Have you heard any imputation to the contrary?

SHYLOCK.

No, no, no, no, no; — my meaning, in saying he is a good man is to have you understand me that he is sufficient. Yet his means are in supposition: he hath an argosy bound to Tripolis, another to the Indies; I understand, moreover, upon the Rialto, he

I.iii

1 **ducats** [ˈdʌkəts]：一种威尼斯金币。

4 **for the which**：for which (which 原为名词，前面可用定冠词)。**bound**：legally engaged to pay back，立约清偿。

6 **May**：can. **stead**(v.)：help. **pleasure**(v.)：gratify，fulfil the wish of.

12 **imputation**：opinion founded on circumstantial evidence，reputation.

15 **sufficient**：solvent，able to pay one's debts，有还债能力的。**supposition**：doubt. **in supposition**：of doubtful existence，open to question.

16 **argosy**：见 I.9 行。 **bound to**：bound for，开赴。 **Tripolis** [ˈtripəlis]：现利比亚首都。

17 **Indies** [ˈindiz]：这里指西印度群岛。 **the Rialto** [riˈæltəu]：威尼斯交易所，一日二市，进行交易和互通情报。

hath a third at Mexico, a fourth for England, — and other ventures he hath, squander'd abroad. But ships are but boards, sailors but men: there be land-rats and water-rats, water-thieves and land-thieves, I mean pirates; and then there is the peril of waters, winds, and rocks. The man is, notwithstanding, sufficient: — three thousand ducats: — I think I may take his bond.

BASSANIO.

Be assured you may.

SHYLOCK.

I will be assured I may; and, that I may be assured, I will bethink me. May I speak with Antonio?

BASSANIO.

If it please you to dine with us.

SHYLOCK.

Yes, to smell pork; to eat of the habitation which your prophet the Nazarite conjured the devil into. I will buy with you, sell with you, talk with you, walk with you, and so following; but I will not eat with you, drink with you, nor pray with you. What news on the Rialto? —Who is he comes here?

Enter ANTONIO

BASSANIO.

This is Signior Antonio.

SHYLOCK [*aside*].

How like a fawning publican he looks!
I hate him for he is a Christian!
But more, for that, in low simplicity,
He lends out money gratis, and brings down
The rate of usance here with us in Venice.
If I can catch him once upon the hip,
I will feed fat the ancient grudge I bear him.
He hates our sacred nation; and he rails,

19 **squandered**：scattered. **But**：only.

26 **Be assured**：rest assured.

27 **will be assured**：will make certain. **that**：in order that.

28 **bethink me**：think it over.

30—31 **Yes**：是啊！（这是反话，意思是不行） **to smell pork**：犹太人不吃猪肉。 **habitation**：dwelling place. **the Nazarite** [ˈnæzərait]：耶稣基督 Jesus Christ，是 Nazareth 出生的人。 **to eat of… the devil into**：去吃你们的拿撒勒先知把魔鬼赶进去的脏东西。见《圣经·新约·马太福音》第 8 章 28—32 节，耶稣使鬼进入猪群。

35 **he comes**：he who comes.

38 **for**：because.

39 **for that**：for the fact that. **low simplicity**：humble ignorance.

40 **gratis** [ˈgreitis]：for nothing，free of charge，免费地，无偿地。

41 **usance**：interest.

42 **catch him**：（摔跤用语）用臀部作支点将他摔倒。

43 **feed fat**：可能意味 more that satify. **ancient grudge**：宿怨。

44 **sacred nation**：the Jews.

Even there where merchants most do congregate,
On me, my bargains, and my well-won thrift,
Which he calls interest. Cursed be my tribe,
If I forgive him!

BASSANIO.

Shylock, do you hear?

SHYLOCK.

I am debating of my present store;
And, by the near guess of my memory,
I cannot instantly raise up the gross
Of full three thousand ducats. What of that?
Tubal, a wealthy Hebrew of my tribe,
Will furnish me. But soft! how many months
Do you desire? —Rest you fair, good signior;
[*to* ANTONIO.
Your worship was the last man in our mouths.

ANTONIO.

Shylock, although I neither lend nor borrow
By taking nor by giving of excess,
Yet, to supply the ripe wants of my friend,
I'll break a custom.— Is he yet possest
How much ye would?

SHYLOCK.

Ay, ay, three thousand ducats.

ANTONIO.

And for three months.

SHYLOCK.

I had forgot,—three months, you told me so.
Well, then, your bond; and let me see,—but hear you;
Methought you said you neither lend nor borrow
Upon advantage.

ANTONIO.

I do never use it.

SHYLOCK.

45 **congregate**: gather.

44—46 **rail, …/On**: rail at, jeer at. **thrift**: profit.

49 **debating**: considering, calculating. **of**: about.

51 **gross**: full sum.

54 **soft**: stay, stop.

55 **Rest you fair**: may you be well.

56 **the last…mouths**: just now talked about by us.

58 **By taking nor by giving of excess**: By the taking or giving of excess. **excess**: interest, i.e. more than the original loan.

59 **ripe wants**: urgent needs.

60 **Is…possest**: has he been informed.

61 **would**: wanted. **Ay**: yes.

63 **forgot**: forgotten.

66 **Upon advantage**: with interest, for profit. **use**: put out at interest.

When Jacob grazed his uncle Laban's sheep,—
This Jacob from our holy Abram was
(As his wise mother wrought in his behalf)
The third possessor; ay, he was the third,—

ANTONIO.

And what of him? did he take interest?

SHYLOCK.

No, not take interest; not as you would say,
Directly interest: mark what Jacob did.
When Laban and himself were compromised
That all the eanlings which were streakt and pied
Should fall as Jacob's hire, the ewes, being rank,
In th'end of autumn turned to the rams;
And when the work of generation was
Between these woolly breeders in the act,
The skilful shepherd peel'd me certain wands,
And, in the doing of the deed of kind,
He stuck them up before the fulsome ewes,
Who, then conceiving, did in eaning time
Fall parti-colour'd lambs, and those were Jacob's.
This was a way to thrive, and he was blest:
And thrift is blessing, if men steal it not.

ANTONIO.

This was a venture, sir, that Jacob served for;
A thing not in his power to bring to pass,
But sway'd and fashion'd by the hand of heaven.
Was this inserted to make interest good?
Or is your gold and silver ewes and rams?

SHYLOCK.

I cannot tell: I make it breed as fast:—
But note me, signior.

ANTONIO.

Mark you this, Bassanio,
The devil can cite Scripture for his purpose.

67 **grazed**：pastured，放牧。 **When Jacob…sheep**：当初雅各替他舅父拉班牧羊(见《圣经·旧约·创世记》第 30 章 27—43 节)。

68 **Abram**：Abraham，亚伯拉罕，犹太人祖先，见《圣经·旧约·创世记》第 17 章起。

69 **As**：so. **wrought…behalf**：exerted her efforts for his benefit，为他尽力。

70 **third possessor**：第三代族长。

74 **compromised**：agreed.

75 **eanlings**：new-born lambs. **streakt and pied**：striped and spotted，有条纹的和有斑点的。

76 **hire** (n.)：pay，工钱。 **ewes**：母羊。 **rank** (adj.)：in heat，发情。

77 **rams**：公羊。

78 **generation**：regeneration，繁殖。

79 **in the act**：in process.

80 **me**：泛指人称与格(ethical dative)，在句中只起加强语气的作用，无实词意义。

81 **kind**：nature，what is bred in the bone，天性，本性。 **the deed of kind**：传宗接代的事。

82 **fulsome**：fat.

83 **eaning time**：lambing season，生小羊的季节。

84 **fall** (v.t.)：let fall，give birth to，生下。

87 **a…for**：a risk (an adventure) that Jacob took，雅各碰的一次运气(冒的一次险)。

89 **sway'd**：swayed，governed，controlled，被控制的。 **fashion'd**：fashioned，shaped，made，被形成的。

90 **make interest good**：justify charging interest，为索取利息作辩护。

92 **as fast**：as fast as Jacob's sheep.

93 **note**：mark，listen to. **Mark**：pay attention to，note.

An evil soul, producing holy witness,
Is like a villain with a smiling cheek;
A goodly apple rotten at the heart:
O, what a goodly outside falsehood hath!

SHYLOCK.

Three thousand ducats,—'tis a good round sum.
Three months from twelve, — then, let me see, the rate—

ANTONIO.

Well, Shylock, shall we be beholden to you?

SHYLOCK.

Signior Antonio, many a time and oft,
In the Rialto, you have rated me
About my moneys and my usances:
Still have I borne it with a patient shrug;
For sufferance is the badge of all our tribe:
You call me misbeliever, cut-throat dog,
And spit upon my Jewish gaberdine,
And all for use of that which is mine own.
Well, then, it now appears you need my help:
Go to, then; you come to me, and you say,
'Shylock, we would have moneys:'—you say so;
You, that did void your rheum upon my beard,
And foot me as you spurn a stranger cur
Over your threshold: moneys is your suit.
What should I say to you? Should I not say,
'Hath a dog money? is it possible
A cur can lend three thousand ducats?' or
Shall I bend low, and in a bondman's key,
With bated breath and whispering humbleness,
Say this,—
'Fair sir, you spit on me on Wednesday last;
You spurn'd me such a day; another time
You call'd me dog; and for these courtesies

95 producing holy witness：引《圣经》为证。

98 goodly outside：good-looking appearance.

99 round sum：整数。

100 twelve：twelve months.

101 beholden：obliged. **shall… you?**：你能不能帮我们这次忙？

103 rated：berated，abused，辱骂。

105 Still：always.

106 sufferance：patience. **badge**：标记，特征。

107 misbeliever：信邪教者。

108 gaberdine [ˈgæbədiːn]：loose cloak or mantle，一种宽大的长袍。

109 And all：and I have suffered all this. **for… own**：for using my own money. **use**：见前 66 行。

111 Go to：very well.

112 moneys：见下 115 行注。

113 void your rheum：spit，吐唾沫。

114 foot (v.t.)：kick. **spurn**：kick. **stranger** (adj.)：strange，belonging to another person.

115 suit (n.)：request. **moneys is**：当时如 money 这样的名词可用复数形式，但仍作单数看待，故 125 行处用 much 修饰。

119 bondman's key：slave's tone，奴才的腔调。

I'll lend you thus much moneys'?

ANTONIO.

I am as like to call thee so again,
To spit on thee again, to spurn thee too.
If thou wilt lend this money, lend it not
As to thy friends—for when did friendship take
A breed for barren metal of his friend? —
But lend it rather to thine enemy;
Who if he break, thou mayst with better face
Exact the penalty.

SHYLOCK.

Why, look you, how you storm!
I would be friends with you, and have your love,
Forget the shames that you have stain'd me with,
Supply your present wants, and take no doit
Of usance for my moneys,
And you'll not hear me: this is kind I offer.

BASSANIO.

This were kindness.

SHYLOCK.

This kindness will I show:—
Go with me to a notary, seal me there
Your single bond; and, in a merry sport,
If you repay me not on such a day,
In such a place, such sum or sums as are
Exprest in the condition, let the forfeit
Be nominated for an equal pound
Of your fair flesh, to be cut off and taken
In what part of your body pleaseth me.

ANTONIO.

Content, i'faith: I'll seal to such a bond,
And say there is much kindness in the Jew.

BASSANIO.

You shall not seal to such a bond for me:

126 **like** (adj.): likely.

130 **breed** (n.): unnatural offspring. **barren metal**: 不能生孩子的金属。按这里 Antonio 引希腊哲学家亚里士多德的意见,认为金银不能生息,所以利息是不合理、不合法的。 **of**: from.

132 **Who**: from whom. **break**: goes bankrupt, 破产。

133 **Exact**: 逼索。 **penalty**: punishment, forfeiture, 罚物。 **storm** (v.): fly into a temper, 发脾气。

135 **shames**: disgraces, 侮辱。 **that ... with**: with which you have stained me.

136 **doit** [dɔit]: small Dutch coin, a trifle.

138 **this is kind I offer**: what I offer is gracious.

139 **were**: would be(虚拟语气,表示怀疑)。

140 **notary**: 公证人。

141 **Your single bond**: the bond of you alone. **merry sport**: jest, spirit of fun,玩笑。

144 **forfeit**: penalty, 因违约而受的罚。

145 **nominated for**: named as. **equal** (adj.): exact, 整整的。

147 In any part of your body which pleases me.

148 **Content** (adj.): agreed, 同意。 **seal to**: sign.

I'll rather dwell in my necessity.

ANTONIO.

Why, fear not, man; I will not forfeit it:
Within these two months, that's a month before
This bond expires, I do expect return
Of thrice three times the value of this bond.

SHYLOCK.

O father Abram, what these Christians are,
Whose own hard dealings teaches them suspect
The thoughts of others! —Pray you, tell me this;
If he should break his day, what should I gain
By the exaction of the forfeiture?
A pound of man's flesh taken from a man
Is not so estimable, profitable neither,
As flesh of muttons, beefs, or goats. I say,
To buy his favour, I extend this friendship:
If he will take it, so; if not, adieu;
And, for my love, I pray you wrong me not.

ANTONIO.

Yes, Shylock, I will seal unto this bond.

SHYLOCK.

Then meet me forthwith at the notary's,—
Give him direction for this merry bond;
And I will go and purse the ducats straight;
See to my house, left in the fearful guard
Of an unthrifty knave; and presently
I will be with you.

ANTONIO.

Hie thee, gentle Jew.

[*Exit* SHYLOCK.

The Hebrew will turn Christian: he grows kind.

BASSANIO.

I like not fair terms and a villain's mind.

ANTONIO.

151 **I'll rather**：I had rather. **dwell**：remain. **necessity**：want (of money).

152 **forfeit**：fail to keep.

156 **what**：what kind of people.

157 注意这里 dealings 的谓语用单数，可能是把 dealings 看作一个单数的概念。 **suspect**：前省略 to.

159 **break his day**：违限。 **day**：time-limit.

160 **exaction**：逼付。 **forfeiture**：被罚之物。

162 **estimable**：valuable.

163 **muttons**：sheep. **beefs**：cows.

165 **so**：very well. **adieu** [法语，əˈdjuː]：goodbye.

166 **for my love**：for my sake，considering my good will.

169 **direction**：instruction. **merry bond**：见上 141 行。

170 **purse**(v.)：put in a purse. **straight**：at once.

171 **fearful**：to be feared，untrustworthy，使人不放心的。**guard**(n.)：照管，守护。

172 **unthrifty**：good-for-nothing，没出息的。 **knave**：（轻蔑语）servant.

173 **Hie**：hasten，去吧。 **gentle**：complimentary epithet.

Come on: in this there can be no dismay;
My ships come home a month before the day.

[*Exeunt*.

177 **day**: day of payment.

ACT II

SCENE I

Belmont. A room in PORTIA'S *house.*

Enter the PRINCE OF MOROCCO, *a tawny Moor, all in white, and three or four* FOLLOWERS *accordingly, with* PORTIA, NERISSA, *and their* TRAIN. *Flourish of cornets.*

PRINCE OF MOROCCO.

Mislike me not for my complexion,
The shadow'd livery of the burnisht sun,
To whom I am a neighbour and near bred.
Bring me the fairest creature northward born,
Where Phœbus' fire scarce thaws the icicles,
And let us make incision for your love,
To prove whose blood is reddest, his or mine.
I tell thee, lady, this aspect of mine
Hath fear'd the valiant: by my love, I swear
The best-regarded virgins of our clime
Hath loved it too: I would not change this hue,
Except to steal your thoughts, my gentle queen.

PORTIA.

In terms of choice I am not solely led
By nice direction of a maiden's eyes;
Besides, the lottery of my destiny
Bars me the right of voluntary choosing:
But, if my father had not scanted me,
And hedg'd me by his will, to yield myself
His wife who wins me by that means I told you,
Yourself, renowned prince, then stood as fair

II.i

tawny ['tɔːni]: brownish-yellow. ***Moor*** [muə]: 摩尔人(指西北非和西班牙的阿拉伯人)。 ***accordingly***: matching. **TRAIN**: body of followers. ***Flourish***: 响亮的吹奏。 ***cornets***: 短号。

1 **Mislike**: dislike.

2 **shadow'd**: dark. **The shadow'd…sun**: complexion 的同位语, dark livery of a servant of the Sun God.

3 **bred**: brought up.

5 **Phœbus** ['fiːbəs]: 希腊神话中的太阳神, 即 Apollo. **scarce**: scarcely.

6 **incision**: blood-letting, 刺血。 **for your love**: for our love of you, 为了你的爱情。

7 **reddest**: 现在说 redder.

8 **aspect**(重音在第二音节): face.

9 **fear'd**: frightened.

10—11 **regarded**: held in respect or honor. **clime**: climate, country. **virgins…/Hath**: 又一个复数主语用单数谓语的例子。

12 **Except** (conj.): unless. **steal your thoughts**: win your love under disguise.

13 **In terms of**: in the way of.

14 **nice**: fastidious, 挑剔的。 **direction**: guidance (介词短语中省略定冠词)。

16 **the right**: 前省略 from.

17 **scanted**: stinted, limited.

18 **hedg'd**: hedged, confined.

19 **His wife who**: wife of the man who.

20 **stood**: would be.

As any comer I have lookt on yet
For my affection.

PRINCE OF MOROCCO.

Even for that I thank your:
Therefore, I pray you, lead me to the caskets,
To try my fortune. By this scimitar,
That slew the Sophy and a Persian prince
That won three fields of Sultan Solyman,
I would outstare the sternest eyes that look,
Outbrave the heart most daring on the earth,
Pluck the young sucking-cubs from the she-bear.
Yea, mock the lion when he roars for prey,
To win thee, lady. But, alas the while!
If Hercules and Lichas play at dice
Which is the better man, the greater throw
May turn by fortune from the weaker hand:
So is Alcides beaten by his page;
And so may I, blind Fortune leading me,
Miss that which one unworthier may attain,
And die with grieving.

PORTIA.

You must take your chance;
And either not attempt to choose at all,
Or swear before you choose,—if you choose wrong,
Never to speak to lady afterward
In way of marriage: therefore be advised.

PRINCE OF MOROCCO.

Nor will not. Come, bring me unto my chance.

PORTIA.

First, forward to the temple: after dinner
Your hazard shall be made.

PRINCE OF MOROCCO.

Good fortune, then!
To make me blest or cursed'st among men.

24 scimitar：阿拉伯和土耳其的弯刀。

25 Sophy [ˈsəufi]：former title of king of Persia (now Iran).

26 fields：battles. **Sultan Solyman**：the Sultan Suleiman I of Turkey (1494—1566) was defeated in Persia in 1535.

27 outstare：stare out of countenance，怒目凝视，直至对方吓得低下头。

28 Outbrave：exceed in bravery.

29 sucking-cubs：吃奶的幼兽。

30 Yea [jei]：yes.

31 the while：the present time. **alas the while!**：(exclamation of grief) 其他如 woe the while，bad world the while 等也都是表示悲哀的感叹语。

32 Hercules [ˈhəːkjuliːs]：希腊罗马神话中的大力英雄赫格立斯。**Lichas** [ˈlitʃəs]：servant and friend of Hercules.

33 Which：to see which.

34 turn … from：掷自。

35 Alcides [ælˈsaidiːz]：Hercules 的别名。 **page**：童仆，小侍从。**So…page**：Hercules 由于穿上了 Lichas 奉主母 Dejanira 之命送来的有毒的内衣，痛苦万分，只好举火自焚。

42 In way of：介词短语中省略定冠词。 **be advised**：consider carefully.

43 Nor will not：(双否定仍表否定)No，I will not (speak to lady with a view to marriage).

44 to the temple：to the church (to take the oath).

45 hazard(n.)：risk，chance.

46 blest or cursed'st：最幸福或最倒运的(第二个词的屈折变化形式'st 表示 blest 和 cursed 两个词的最高级，这是莎士比亚时代一种特殊的语法现象)。

[*Cornets, and exeunt.*

SCENE II

Venice. A street.

Enter LAUNCELOT *the Clown, alone.*

LAUNCELOT GOBBO.

Certainly my conscience will serve me to run from this Jew my master. The fiend is at mine elbow, and tempts me, saying to me, 'Gobbo, Launcelot Gobbo, good Launcelot,' or 'good Gobbo,' or 'good Launcelot Gobbo, use your legs, take the start, run away.' My conscience says, 'No; take heed, honest Launcelot; take heed, honest Gobbo,' or, as aforesaid, 'honest Launcelot Gobbo; do not run; scorn running with thy heels.' Well, the most courageous fiend bids me pack: '*Via!*' says the fiend, 'away!' says the fiend; 'for the heavens, rouse up a brave mind,' says the fiend, 'and run.' Well, my conscience, hanging about the neck of my heart, says very wisely to me, 'My honest friend Launcelot, being an honest man's son,' — or rather an honest woman's son; — for, indeed, my father did something smack, something grow to, — he had a kind of taste; — well, my conscience says, 'Launcelot, budge not.' 'Budge,' says the fiend. 'Budge not,' says my conscience. 'Conscience,' say I, 'you counsel well; fiend,' say I, 'you counsel well:' to be ruled by my conscience, I should stay with the Jew my master, who — God bless the mark! — is a kind of devil; and, to run away from the Jew, I should be ruled by the fiend, who, saving your reverence, is the devil himself. Certainly the Jew is the very devil incarnal; and, in

II.ii

GOBBO：在意大利语意为"驼背"，他是个扮成驼背的小丑。

1 **conscience**：sense of right and wrong. **serve me to run**：give me my deserts for running.

5 **take the start**：start off，开始跑。

7—8 **as aforesaid**：as I said before. **scorn**：abstain from.

10 **pack**：depart with one's belongings. ***Via***！［意大利语，viə］：away.

11—12 **for the heavens**：for heaven's sake. **rouse up a brave mind**：pluck up courage.

13 **hanging about the neck**：像孩子用手勾住妈妈的脖子。

16 **smack** (v.i.)：have a bad taste (of lechery).

17 **something** (adv.)：somewhat. **grow to**：（牛奶）巴锅（的焦味）。 **have a kind of taste**：有异味。

19 **Budge**：move.

21 **ruled**：governed.

22—23 **God bless the mark!**：save the mark，excuse my (unpleasant) remark.

25 **saving your reverence**：apology for unseemly expression.

26 **incarnal**：为 incarnate 之误，意为"化身"(Gobbo 父子均系不学无术之人，但都喜用"大字"而且经常用错)。

my conscience, my conscience is but a kind of hard conscience, to offer to counsel me to stay with the Jew. The fiend gives the more friendly counsel: I will run, fiend; my heels are at your command; I will run.

Enter OLD GOBBO, *with a basket*.

OLD GOBBO.

Master young man, you, I pray you, which is the way to master Jew's?

LAUNCELOT GOBBO [*aisde*].

O heavens, this is my true-begotten father! who, being more than sand-blind, high-gravel-blind, knows me not:—I will try confusions with him.

OLD GOBBO.

Master young gentleman, I pray you, which is the way to master Jew's?

LAUNCELOT GOBBO.

Turn up on your right hand at the next turning, but, at the next turning of all, on your left; marry, at the very next turning, turn of no hand, but turn down indirectly to the Jew's house.

OLD GOBBO.

By God's sonties, 'twill be a hard way to hit. Can you tell me whether one Launcelot, that dwells with him, dwell with him or no?

LAUNCELOT GOBBO.

Talk you of young Master Launcelot? — [*aside*] Mark me now; now will I raise the waters. — Talk you of young Master Launcelot?

OLD GOBBO.

No master, sir, but a poor man's son: his father, though I say it, is an honest exceeding poor man, and, God be thankt, well to live.

LAUNCELOT GOBBO.

26—27 in my conscience：to my mind.

36 true-begotten：亲生的。

37 sand-blind：half-blind，dim-sighted. **high-gravel-blind**：几乎全瞎。

38 try confusions with：try to confuse.

42 marry（一种惊叹词）：by the Virgin Mary.

43—44 turn of no hand：既不向左，又不向右。这里 of 等于 on. **turn down indirectly to…**：间接地转到…，七转八转地转到…。

45 sonties：saints. **hit**：find.

48 Master：（尊称）Mr.

49 raise the waters：bring tears to his eyes.

52 though I say it：excuse me for saying it，恕我这么说。 **exceeding**：exceedingly，very.

53 well to live：well to do.

Well, let his father be what a' will, we talk of young Master Launcelot.

OLD GOBBO.

Your worship's friend, and Launcelot, sir.

LAUNCELOT GOBBO.

But, I pray you, *ergo*, old man, *ergo*, I beseech you, talk you of young Master Launcelot?

OLD GOBBO.

Of Launcelot, an't please your mastership.

LAUNCELOT GOBBO.

Ergo, Master Launcelot. Talk not of Master Launcelot, father; for the young gentleman — according to Fates and Destinies, and such odd sayings. the Sisters Three, and such branches of learning — is, indeed, deceased; or, as you would say in plain terms, gone to heaven.

OLD GOBBO.

Marry, God forbid! the boy was the very staff of my age, my very prop.

LAUNCELOT GOBBO.

Do I look like a cudgel or a hovel-post, a staff, or a prop?— Do you know me, father?

OLD GOBBO.

Alack the day, I know you not, young gentleman: but, I pray you, tell me, is my boy — God rest his soul! —alive or dead?

LAUNCELOT GOBBO.

Do you not know me, father?

OLD GOBBO.

Alack, sir, I am sand-blind; I know you not.

LAUNCELOT GOBBO.

Nay, indeed, if you had your eyes, you might fail of the knowing me: it is a wise father that knows

54 **a'**：ha 旧时 he 的一种口语省读形式。

56 **You…friend**：前面省 I am. **Your worship**：（尊称）大人，老爷。 **and Launcelot**：i.e. plain Launcelot，not Master Launcelot.

57 ***ergo***〈拉丁语〉：therefore.

59 **an't**：if it.

62—63 **Sisters Three**：希腊神话中的三个命运女神：Clotho，Lachesis and Atropos.

66 **staff**：拐杖。

68 **hovel-post**：post supporting a hovel.

70 **Alack the day**：alas.

71—72 **God rest his soul!**：上帝让他的灵魂安息吧！

74 **Alack**：alas.

75—76 **fail of the knowing**：fail to know.

his own child. Well, old man, I will tell you news of your son: give me your blessing [*kneels*]: truth will come to light; murder cannot be hid long, — a man's son may; but, in the end, truth will out.

OLD GOBBO.

Pray you, sir, stand up: I am sure you are not Launcelot, my boy.

LAUNCELOT GOBBO.

Pray you, let's have no more fooling about it, but give me your blessing: I am Launcelot, your boy that was, your son that is, your child that shall be.

OLD GOBBO.

I cannot think you are my son.

LAUNCELOT GOBBO.

I know not what I shall think of that: but I am Launcelot, the Jew's man; and I am sure Margery your wife is my morther.

OLD GOBBO.

Her name is Margery, indeed: I'll be sworn, if thou be Launcelot, thou art mine won flesh and blood. Lord worshipt might he be! what a beard hast thou got! thou hast got more hair on thy chin than Dobbin my fill-horse has on his tail.

LAUNCELOT GOBBO [*rising*].

It should seem, then, that Dobbin's tail grows backward; I am sure he had more hair of his tail than I have of my face when I last saw him.

OLD GOBBO.

Lord, how art thou changed! How dost thou and thy master agree? I have brought him a present. How 'gree you now?

LAUNCELOT GOBBO.

Well, well: but, for mine own part, as I have set up my rest to run away, so I will not rest till I have

76—87 it is a wise father that knows his own child：这是把谚语"'Tis a wise child that knows his own father"反过来说。

79—80 a man's son may：be hidden long. **man**：servant.

90 thou：老 Gobbo 在确知 Launcelot 是其子时，对他从 you 改称 thou.

92—93 Lord worshipt might he be!：May Lord be worshiped! **what a beard hast thou got!**：Launcelot has knelt with his back to his father，who feels his long hair and thinks it is a beard.

94 fill-horse：cart horse.

95—96 grows backward：越来越短。 **of**：on.

98—99 How dost thou and thy master agree?：你跟你的东家合得来么?

100 'gree：agree.

101—102 set up my rest：decided to risk everything. **rest**：the stakes kept in reserve in gambling.

run some ground. My master's a very Jew: give him a present! give him a halter: I am famisht in his service; you may tell every finger I have with my ribs. Father, I am glad you are come: give me your present to one Master Bassanio, who, indeed, gives rare new liveries: if I serve not him, I will run as far as God has any ground. — O rare fortune! here comes the man: — to him, father; for I am a Jew, if I serve the Jew any longer.

Enter BASSANIO, *with* LEONARDO *and a* FOLLOWER *or two.*

BASSANIO.

You may do so; — but let it be so hasted, that supper be ready at the furthest by five of the clock. See these letters deliver'd; put the liveries to making; and desire Gratiano to come anon to my lodging.

[*Exit a* SERVANT.

LAUNCELOT GOBBO.

To him, father.

OLD GOBBO.

God bless your worship!

BASSANIO.

Gramercy: wouldst thou aught with me?

OLD GOBBO.

Here's my son, sir, a poor boy,—

LAUNCELOT GOBBO.

Not a poor boy, sir, but the rich Jew's man; that would, sir, —as my father shall specify,—

OLD GOBBO.

He hath a great infection, sir, as one would say, to serve,—

LAUNCELOT GOBBO.

Indeed, the short and the long is, I serve the Jew, and have a desire,—as my father shall specify,—

103 **ground**：distance. **a very Jew**：a Jew in every respect.

104 **halter**：noose，上吊的绳子。

105—106 **tell**：count. **you may tell every fiuger I have with my ribs**：你可以用我的肋骨数出我的每一个手指来(Launcelot 说这话时将手放在胸前,拿着父亲的手摸自己的手指,要使他误以为摸到的真是根肋骨)。

106 **me**：语气词(无词汇意义,泛指的人称与格)。

108 **rare new**：very new.

110 **am**：will become. **I am a Jew，if…**：又是一种表否定的句式。

112 **hasted** ['heistid]：hastened.

113—114 **furthest**：latest. **of the clock**：o'clock. In Elizabethan England they dined about 11 a.m. and supped about 5 p.m. **See these letters deliver'd**：see (to it) that these letters are delivered.

115 **anon**：at once，soon.

118 **Gramercy** [grə'məːsi]：〈古法语〉grant merci，等于 (God give you) great reward. **wouldst thou**：do you want. **aught**：anything.

121 **specify**：point out.

125 **infection**：系 affection (desire)之误。

OLD GOBBO.

His master and he — saving your worship's reverence —are scarce cater-cousins,—

LAUNCELOT GOBBO.

To be brief, the very truth is, that the Jew having done me wrong, doth cause me, — as my father, being, I hope, an old man, shall frutify unto you,—

OLD GOBBO.

I have here a dish of doves that I would bestow upon your worship;and my suit is,—

LAUNCELOT GOBBO.

In very brief, the suit is impertinent to myself, as your worship shall know by this honest old man; and, though I say it, though old man, yet poor man, my father.

BASSANIO.

One speak for both. —What would you?

LAUNCELOT GOBBO.

Serve you, sir.

OLD GOBBO.

That is the very defect of the matter, sir.

BASSANIO.

I know thee well; thou hast obtain'd thy suit:
Shylock thy master spoke with me this day,
And hath preferr'd thee, —if it be preferment
To leave a rich Jew's service, to become
The follower of so poor a gentleman.

LAUNCELOT GOBBO.

The old proverb is very well parted between my master Shylock and you, sir: you have the grace of God, sir, and he hath enough.

BASSANIO.

Thou speak'st it well. — Go, father, with thy son. —
Take leave of thy old master, and inquire

131 **are … cater-cousins**：are not closely related, do not often agree. **scarce**：scarcely. **cater-cousins**：table companions.

134 **frutify**：系 certify(证实)之误。

135—136 **bestow/upon**：赏给(用词不当)。 **suit**：request.

137 **impertinen**：系 pertinent(关于)之误。

142 **defect**：系 effect(主旨)之误。

145 **preferr'd thee**：recommended you for advancement. **preferment**：晋升。

148 **The old proverb**："He that hath the grace of God, hath enough." **parted**：divided.

151 **it**：无特指的宾语。

My lodging out.—Give him a livery
More guarded than his fellows': see it done.

LAUNCELOT GOBBO.

Father, in. — I cannot get a service, no; — I have ne, er a tongue in my head. — Well [*looking on his palm*], if any man in Italy have a fairer table, which doth offer to swear upon a book, I shall have good fortune! — Go to, here's a simple line of life! here's a small trifle of wives! alas, fifteen wives is nothing! eleven widows and nine maids is a simple coming-in for one man; and then to scape drowning thrice, and to be in peril of my life with the edge of a feather-bed, — here are simple scapes! Well, if Fortune be a woman, she's a good wench for this gear. — Father, come; I'll take my leave of the Jew in the twinkling of an eye.

[*Exeunt* LAUNCELOT *and* OLD GOBBO.

BASSANIO.

I pray thee, good Leonardo, think on this:
These things being bought and orderly bestow'd,
Return in haste, for I do feast to-night
My best-esteem'd acquaintance: hie thee, go.

LEONARDO.

My best endeavours shall be done herein.

Enter GRATIANO.

GRATIANO.

Where's your master?

LEONARDO.

Yonder, sir, he walks. [*Exit*.

GRATIANO.

signior Bassanio,—

BASSANIO.

Gratiano!

GRATIANO.

154 **More guarded**：trimmed with more braid，镶更多边的。

157 **table**：lines in the palm，(看手相的)掌纹。 **which**：who.

158 **book**：Bible. **swear upon a book**：手按《圣经》发誓。

159 **Go to**：相当于 come，表示难以置信的感叹词。下面一段说的是他自己的手相。 **line of life**：拇指根上的圆形，表生命。

159，161，164 **simple**：poor or small.

160 **small trifle of**：small number of.

162 **coming-in**：income (in the form of dowries). **scape**(v.)：escape.

163—164 **in peril of my life with the edge of a feather-bed**：差点被羽绒被的一角闷死。

164 **scapes** (n.)：escapes.

166 **gear**：sort of thing.

168 **think on**：think of.

169 **bestow'd**：stowed in the hold (of the ship bound for Belmont).

170 **feast** (v.t.)：宴请。

171 **acquaintance**：(当时可作集合名词用) acquaintances. **hie**：hasten.

I have a suit to you.

BASSANIO.

You have obtain'd it.

GRATIANO.

You must not deny me: I must go with you to
Belmont.

BASSANIO.

Why, then you must. But hear thee, Gratiano:
Thou art too wild, too rude, and bold of voice,—
Parts that become thee happily enough,
And in such eyes as ours appear not faults;
But where thou art not known, why, there they show
Something too liberal. Prithee, take pain
To allay with some cold drops of modesty
Thy skipping spirtit; lest, through thy wild behaviour,
I be misconstred in the place I go to,
And lose my hopes.

GRATIANO.

Signior Bassanio, hear me:
If I do not put on a sober habit,
Talk with respect, and swear but now and then,
Wear prayer-books in my pocket, look demurely;
Nay, more, while grace is saying, hood mine eyes
Thus with my hat, and sigh, and say amen;
Use all the observance of civility,
Like one well studied in a sad ostent
To please his grandam, —never trust me more.

BASSANIO.

Well, we shall see your bearing.

GRATIANO.

Nay, but I bar to-night: you shall not gauge me
By what we do to-night.

BASSANIO.

No, that were pity:

176 **a suit to you**：a favor to ask of you.

179 **hear thee**：祈使语气的 hear 之后，用非强调的代词 thee，这是当时的习惯用法。而且 Bassanio 对 Gratiano 进行批评教导时，换用 thou 的称呼，不再用 you.

181 **Parts**：traits of character，性格，特性。 **happily**：well.

184 **Something** (adv.)：somewhat. **liberal**：unrestrained，free and easy. **Prithee**：(I) pray thee，please. **take pain**：现在说 take pains.

185 **modesty**：moderation，节删。

186 **skipping**：flighty，thoughtless.

187 **misconstred**：misconstrued，misunderstood.

189 **habit**：appearance，deportment，外表，仪态。 **put on a sober habit**：assume an air of gravity.

190 **with respect**：with respectability，庄重地。 **but**：only.

191 **demurely**：soberly，gravely.

192 **Nay**：not only this，furthermore，不仅如此。 **grace**：饭前后感恩祷告。 **is saying**：is being said.

193 **amen**：基督教祈祷结束时的附和祝愿语。

194 **observance**：performance of ritual or custom. **civility**：good breeding，polite behavior.

195 **sad ostent**：serious appearance.

196 **grandam**：祖母。

197 **bearing**：conduct，举止。

198 **Nay**：no 进一步强调前面所说的 never trust me more. **bar**：exclude. **gauge** [geidʒ] (v.)：measure，judge of.

199 **were pity**：would be a pity.

I would entreat you rather to put on
Your boldest suit of mirth, for we have friends
That purpose merriment. But fare ye well:
I have some business.

GRATIANO.

And I must to Lorenzo and the rest:
But we will visit you at supper-time. [*Exeunt*.

SCENE III

The same. A room in SHYLOCK'S *house*.

Enter JESSICA *and* LAUNCELOT.

JESSICA.

I am sorry thou wilt leave my father so:
Our house is hell: and thou, a merry devil,
Didst rob it of some taste of tediousness.
But fare thee well; there is a ducat for thee:
And, Launcelot, soon at supper shalt thou see
Lorenzo, who is thy new master's guest:
Give him this letter; do it secretly;—
And so farewell: I would not have my father
See me in talk with thee.

LAUNCELOT GOBBO.

Adieu; tears exhibit my tongue. Most beautiful pagan, most sweet Jew! if a Christian did not play the knave and get thee, I am much deceived. But, adieu: these foolish drops do something drown my manly spirit: adieu.

JESSICA.

Farewell, good Launcelot.— [*Exit* LAUNCELOT.
Alack, what heinous sin is it in me
To be ashamed to be my father's child!
But though I am a daughter to his blood,

201 **suit**：dress，apparel (转义 appearance).

202 **purpose merriment**：intend to have a good time.

204 **must to**：must go to.

II.iii

3 **rob**：rid.

10 **exhibit**：系 inhibit (restrain)之误。

11—12 **did not play the knave and get thee**：不曾和你妈偷情而生下你。 **get**：beget，give birth to.

13 **drops**：tears. **something** (adv.)：somewhat.

I am not to his manners. O Lorenzo,
If thou keep promise, I shall end this strife,—
Become a Christian; and thy loving wife! [*Exit*.

SCENE IV

The same. A street.

Enter GRATIANO, LORENZO, SALARINO, *and* SOLANIO.

LORENZO.
Nay, we will slink away in supper-time,
Disguise us at my lodging, and return
All in an hour.

GRATIANO.
We have not made good preparation.

SALARINO.
We have not spoke us yet of torch-bearers.

SOLANIO.
'Tis vile, unless it may be quaintly order'd,
And better in my mind not undertook.

LORENZO.
'Tis now but four o'clock: we have two hours
To furnish us.

Enter LAUNCELOT, *with a letter*.

Friend Launcelot, what's the news?

LAUNCELOT GOBBO.
An it shall please you to break up this, it shall seem to signify.

LORENZO.
I know the hand: in faith, 'tis a fair hand;
And whiter than the paper it writ on
Is the fair hand that writ.

GRATIANO.
Love-news, in faith.

19 **manners**：morals，moral character.

20 **strife**：state of conflict.

II.iv

1 **in**：at.

2 **Disguise us**：disguise ourselves，化装以参加假面舞会。

5 **spoke us…of**：spoken for ourselves about，bespoken (ordered) for ourselves (spoke 为旧时过去分词形式)，为我们自己定雇了。

6 **vile**：poor，cheap. **may**：can. **quaintly order'd**：ingeniously arranged.

7 **undertook**：undertaken.

9 **furnish us**：equip ourselves.

10 **An**：if. **break up**：open by breaking the seal. **shall**：为假设语气。

14 **writ**：wrote.

15 **in faith**：really.

LAUNCELOT GOBBO.

By your leave, sir.

LORENZO.

Whither goest thou?

LAUNCELOT GOBBO.

Marry, sir, to bid my old master the Jew to sup to-night with my new master the Christian.

LORENZO.

Hold here, take this[*gives money*]:—tell gentle Jessica
I will not fail her; speak it privately; go.—
[*Exit* LAUNCELOT.
Gentlemen, will you prepare you for this mask to-night?
I am provided of a torch-bearer.

SALARINO.

Ay, marry, I'll be gone about it straight.

SOLANIO.

And so will I.

LORENZO.

Meet me and Gratiano
At Gratiano's lodging some hour hence.

SALARINO.

'Tis good we do so. [*Exeunt* SALARINO *and* SOLANIO.

GRATIANO.

Was not that letter from fair Jessica?

LORENZO.

I must needs tell thee all. She hath directed
How I shall take her from her father's house;
What gold and jewels she is furnisht with;
What page's suit she hath in readiness,
If e'er the Jew her father come to heaven,
It will be for his gentle daughter's sake:
And never dare misfortune cross her foot,
Unless she do it under this excuse,—

16 **By your leave**：with your permission (I'll go now).

18 **sup**：have supper.

20 **Hold here**：wait a minute.

22 **prepare you**：prepare yourselves. **mask**：masquerade ball in which dancing，music and pantomine play a part，假面舞会。

24 **provided of**：provided with.

25 **be gone about it**：go (or set) about it. **straight**：immediately.

27 **some hour hence**：about an hour from now.

30 **must needs**：must，needs 为副词，用在 must 之后以加强语气。**directed**：given directions.

34 **e'er**：ever.

35 **for his daughter's sake**：on account of his daughter.

36 **dare**：will dare. **cross her foot**：cross her path.

37 **she**：代 misfortune.

That she is issue to a faithless Jew.
Come, go with me: peruse this as thou goest:
Fair Jessica shall be my torch-bearer. [*Exeunt*.

SCENE V

The same. Before SHYLOCK'S *house.*

Enter SHYLOCK *and* LAUNCELOT.

SHYLOCK.

Well, thou shalt see, thy eyes shall be thy judge,
The difference of old Shylock and Bassanio:—
What, Jessica! —thou shalt not gormandize,
As thou hast done with me;—what, Jessica! —
And sleep and snore, and rend apparel out;—
Why, Jessica, I say!

LAUNCELOT GOBBO.

Why, Jessica!

SHYLOCK.

Who bids thee call? I do not bid thee call.

LAUNCELOT GOBBO.

Your worship was wont to tell me that I could do nothing without bidding.

Enter JESSICA.

JESSICA.

Call you? what is your will?

SHYLOCK.

I am bid forth to supper, Jessica:
There are my keys. —But wherefore should I go?
I am not bid for love; they flatter me:
But yet I'll go in hate, to feed upon
The prodigal Christian. —Jessica, my girl,
Look to my house. —I am right loth to go:
There is some ill a-brewing towards my rest,

38 **she**：代 Jessica. **issue**：child，offspring，后裔。 **faithless**：unbelieving，不信基督教的。

39 **peruse**：read.

40 **shall be**：is to be.

II.v

2 **of**：between.

3 **gormandize**：overeat.

5 **rend apparel out**：扯破衣服。

8 **was wont to**：used to.

11 **bid**：bidden，invited.

15 **prodigal**：浪费的，乱花钱的。

16 **Look to**：look after. **right loth**：very reluctant.

17 **ill**：mischief，misfortune. **a-brewing**：brewing，酝酿着。 **towards**：to，against.

For I did dream of money-bags to-night.

LAUNCELOT GOBBO.

I beseech you, sir, go: my young master doth expect your reproach.

SHYLOCK.

So do I his.

LAUNCELOT GOBBO.

And they have conspired together, — I will not say you shall see a mask; but if you do, then it was not for nothing that my nose fell a-bleeding on Black-Monday last at six o'clock i' th' morning, falling out that year on Ash-Wednesday was four year, in th' afternoon.

SHYLOCK.

What, are there masks? —Hear you me, Jessica:
Lock up my doors; and when you hear the drum,
And the vile squealing of the wry-neckt fife,
Clamber not you up to the casements then,
Nor thrust your head into the public street,
To gaze on Christian fools with varnisht faces;
But stop my house's ears, I mean my casements:
Let not the sound of shallow foppery enter
My sober house.—By Jacob's staff, I swear
I have no mind of feasting forth to-night:
But I will go.—Go you before me, sirrah;
Say I will come.

LAUNCELOT GOBBO.

I will go before, sir.—
Mistress, look out at window for all this;
There will come a Christian by
Will be worth a Jewess' eye. [*Exit*.

SHYLOCK.

What says that fool of Hagar's offspring, ha?

JESSICA.

18 dream of money-bags：对梦的解释或正或反，如梦见钱袋，可能预示获得或失去钱袋。 **to-night**：last night.

20 reproach：系 approach 之误，但下行 Shylock 则按 reproach 理解。

21 So do I his：So do I expect his reproach.

24—25 my nose fell a-bleeding：鼻子出血被认为是一种征兆。 **Black-Monday**：复活节（每年春分月圆后第一个星期日）的次日叫 Black-Monday，传统认为不吉利。

25—26 falling out：happening，刚好是。 **Ash-Wednesday was four year**：It was four years ago last Ash Wednesday，那是四年前的圣灰节星期三。

30 wry-neckt fife：fife-player holding his neck awry，歪颈的吹笛者（这是 fife 代替 fifer 的转喻）。

33 varnisht faces：painted faces or masks.

35 foppery：foolishness，愚蠢的作乐。

36 by Jacob's staff：凭雅各的节杖（参见《圣经·旧约·创世记》第 32 章 10 节，《圣经·新约·希伯来书》第 11 章 21 节）。

37 of feasting：for feasting. **forth**：out；away from home.

38 sirrah：招呼下属的用语。

41 for all this：in spite of all his words.

42 There will come along a Christian who.

43 Will…eye：双关语 1.from the proverb 'worth a Jew's eye', meaning 'precious'；2.值得犹太女郎的青睐。

44 Hagar's offspring：outcasts (Hagar and her son Ishmael were driven into the desert，见《圣经·旧约·创世记》第 12 章 14 节)。

His words were, 'Farewell, mistress;' nothing else.

SHYLOCK.

The patch is kind enough; but a huge feeder,
Snail-slow in profit, and he sleeps by day
More than the wild-cat: drones hive not with me;
Therefore I part with him; and part with him
To one that I would have him help to waste
His borrow'd purse.—Well, Jessica, go in:
Perhaps I will return immediately:
Do as I bid you; shut doors after you:
Fast bind, fast find,—
A proverb never stale in thrifty mind. [*Exit*.

JESSICA.

Farewell; and if my fortune be not crost,
I have a father, you a daughter, lost. [*Exit*.

SCENE VI

The same.

Enter the Maskers GRATIANO *and* SALARINO.

GRATIANO.

This is the pent-house under which Lorenzo
Desired us to make stand.

SALARINO.

His hour is almost past.

GRATIANO.

And it is marvel he out-dwells his hour,
For lovers ever run before the clock.

SALARINO.

O, ten times faster Venus' pigeons fly
To seal love's bonds new-made than they are wont
To keep obliged faith unforfeited!

GRATIANO.

46 **patch**：fool. **feeder**：eater.

47 **Snail-slow**：slow like a snail. **profit**：progress in learning.

48 **drones**：雄蜂(转义懒汉、寄生虫)。 **hive not**：shall not hive，不要来做窠。

49 **part with**：give up，discharge.

51 **purse**：money.

52 **Perhaps I will**：if possible；I intend to.

54 **Fast bind，fast find**：(谚语) What you bind fast you will find fast，"关得牢，找得快"。

56 **crost**：crossed，thwarted.

57 **have…，lost**：would lose.

II.vi

1 **pent-house**：lean-to，shed attached to a building.

2 **make stand**：take our stand. **hour**：appointed time.

3 **marvel** (n.)：a wonder. **out-dwells**：outstays.

5 **Venus' pigeons**：希腊神话中的爱情女神以鸽群驾车。

6 **wont**：accustomed.

7 **obliged faith**：pledged marriage oath. **unforfeited**：unviolated.

That ever holds: who riseth from a feast
With that keen appetite that he sits down?
Where is the horse that doth untread again
His tedious measures with the unbated fire
That he did pace them first? All things that are,
Are with more spirit chased than enjoy'd.
How like a younker or a prodigal
The scarfed bark puts from her native bay,
Hugg'd and embraced by the strumpet wind!
How like a prodigal doth she return,
With over-weather'd ribs, and ragged sails,
Lean, rent, and beggar'd by the strumpet wind!

SALARINO.

Here comes Lorenzo: —more of this hereafter.

Enter LORENZO.

LORENZO.

Sweet friends, your patience for my long abode;
Not I, but my affairs, have made you wait:
When you shall please to play the thieves for wives,
I'll watch as long for you then.—Approach;
Here dwells my father Jew. —Ho! who's within?

Enter JESSICA, *above*, *in boy's clothes*.

JESSICA.

Who are you? Tell me, for more certainty,
Albeit I'll swear that I do know your tongue.

LORENZO.

Lorenzo, and thy love.

JESSICA.

Lorenzo, certain; and my love, indeed,—
For who love I so much? And now who knows
But you, Lorenzo, whether I am yours?

LORENZO.

Heaven and thy thoughts are witness that thou art.

10 **untread**: retrace.

11 **tedious measures**: tiresome steps. **unbated**: unabated, undiminished. **fire**: fervor, spirit.

14 **younker**: young man, younger son. **prodigal**: 阔少,浪子。

15 **scarfed**: decked out with flags. **bark**: ship. **puts from**: starts from, 开始从…驶出。

16 **Hugg'd**: embraced. **strumpet**: 娼妓,参见《圣经·新约·路加福音》第 15 章 30 节。 **strumpet wind**: 轻狂的风。

18 **over-weather'd**: too much worn-out by storms and waves.

19 **rent** (p.p.): torn.

20 **more of this hereafter**: (We will talk) more about this later on.

21 **your patience**: (thank you for) your indulgence. **abode**: delay.

23 **for wives**: to get wives.

24 **watch**: watch out,守望。

25 **father**: father-in-law.

27 **Albeit**: althouth.

30 **who love I**: whom do I love.

JESSICA.

Here, catch this casket;it is worth the pains.
I am glad 'tis night, you do not look on me,
For I am much ashamed of my exchange:
But love is blind, and lovers cannot see
The pretty follies that themselves commit;
For if they could, Cupid himself would blush
To see me thus transformed to a boy.

LORENZO.

Descend, for you must be my torch-bearer.

JESSICA.

What,must I hold a candle to my shames?
They in themselves, good sooth, are too-too light.
Why, 'tis an office of discovery, love;
And I should be obscured.

LORENZO.

So are you, sweet,
Even in the lovely garnish of a boy.
But come at once;
For the close night doth play the runaway,
And we are stay'd for at Bassanio's feast.

JESSICA.

I will make fast the doors, and gild myself
With some moe ducats, and be with you straight.

[*Exit above*.

GRATIANO.

Now, by my hood, a Gentile, and no Jew.

LORENZO.

Beshrew me but I love her heartily;
For she is wise, if I can judge of her;
And fair she is, if that mine eyes be true;
And true she is, as she hath proved herself;
And therefore, like herself, wise, fair, and true,

33 **pains**: efforts, labour, 辛劳。

35 **exchange**: change of clothes.

40 **must be**: are to be.

41 **shames** (n.): 害羞的事。

42 **good sooth**: in truth, really. **light**: 双关语 1. frivolous; 2. glaring.

43 **office of discovery**: business (of a torch-bearer) to reveal things.

44 **should be**: ought to be . **obscured**: hidden, kept in the dark.

45 **garnish**: garb, attire, 装束。

47 **close**: secret, favorable to concealment, 隐蔽的，秘密的。 **play the runaway**: is slipping away.

48 **stay'd**: waited.

49 **make fast**: fasten, 关好。 **gild**: supply with gold.

50 **moe**: more.

51 **by my hood**: a mild oath. **Gentile**: 非犹太人。

52 **Beshrew me**: curse me, plague on me (为表强调的赌咒用语，常带诙谐)。 **but**: if ... not.

54 **if that**: if. **be true**: do not deceive me.

57 **constant**: loyal, faithful.

Shall she be placed in my constant soul.

Enter JESSICA, *below*.

What, art thou come? — On, gentlemen; away!
Our masking mates by this time for us stay.

[*Exit with* JESSICA *and* SALARINO.

Enter ANTONIO.

ANTONIO.

Who's there?

GRATIANO.

Signior Antonio!

ANTONIO.

Fie, fie, Gratiano! where are all the rest?
'Tis nine o'clock; our friends all stay for you.
No mask to-night: the wind is come about;
Bassanio presently will go aboard:
I have sent twenty out to seek for you.

GRATIANO.

I am glad on't: I desire no more delight
Than to be under sail and gone to-night. [*Exeunt*.

SCENE VII

Belmont. *A room in* PORTIA'S *house*.

Enter PORTIA *with the* PRINCE OF MOROCCO, *and their* TRAINS. *Flourish of cornets*.

PORTIA.

Go draw aside the curtains, and discover
The several caskets to this noble prince.—
Now make your choice.

PRINCE OF MOROCCO.

The first, of gold, which this inscription bears,—
'Who chooseth me shall gain what many men desire;'

59 **mates**: companions, friends. **stay**: wait.
62 **fie**: (an exclamation of impatience) 咄！嗨！
64 **is come about**: has changed.
67 **on't**: of it ('on' and 'of' are often interchanged).
68 **under sail**: 扬帆出航。

II.vii

Flourish: 奏乐。
1 **discover**: reveal, disclose.
4 **inscription**: 题词。 **bears**: carries,载有。

The second, silver, which this promise carries,—
'Who chooseth me shall get as much as he deserves;'
This third, dull lead, with warning all as blunt,—
'Who chooseth me must give and hazard all he hath.'—
How shall I know if I do choose the right?

PORTIA.

The one of them contains my picture, prince:
If you choose that, then I am yours withal.

PRINCE OF MOROCCO.

Some god direct my judgement! Let me see;
I will survey the inscriptions back again.
What says this leaden casket?
'Who chooseth me must give and hazard all he hath.'
Must give, —for what? for lead? hazard for lead?
This casket threatens: men that hazard all
Do it in hope of fair advantages:
A golden mind stoops not to shows of dross;
I'll then nor give nor hazard aught for lead.
What says the silver, with her virgin hue?
'Who chooseth me, shall get as much as he deserves.'
As much as he deserves! —Pause there, Morocco,
And weigh thy value with an even hand:
If thou be'st rated by thy estimation,
Thou dost deserve enough; and yet enough
May not extend so far as to the lady:
And yet to be afeard of my deserving,
Were but a weak disabling of myself.
As much as I deserve! —Why, that's the lady:
I do in birth deserve her, and in fortunes,
In graces, and in qualities of breeding;
But more than these, in love I do deserve.
What if I stray'd no further, but chose here? —
Let's see once more this saying graved in gold:
'Who chooseth me shall gain what many men desire.'

8 **all as blunt**: completely as blunt as lead.

9 **hazard**: risk.

10 **if**: whether. **the right**: the right casket.

12 **withal**: therewith, together with that.

13 **Some…judgement!**: 前面省略 may.

14 **back again**: from the last to the first.

19 **advantages**: profits, interests.

20 **shows of dross**: worthless-seeming objects.

21 **aught**: anything.

22 **virgin hue**: whiteness, color of the moon.

24 **Morocco**: Prince of Morocco (当时常用国名代国王,为转喻 metonymy).

25 **with an even hand**: even-handedly, impartially.

26 **rated**: valued, 估价。 **by thy estimation**: according to your worth.

29 **afeared**: afraid.

30 **weak disabling**: undervaluation, depreciation.

32 **birth**: 门第。 **fortunes**: 财富。

33 **graces**: 人品,风度。 **breeding**: 教养,修养。

36 **graved**: engraved.

Why, that's the lady; all the world desires her;
From the four corners of the earth they come,
To kiss this shrine, this mortal-breathing saint:
The Hyrcanian deserts and the vasty wilds
Of wide Arabia are as throughfares now
For princes to come view fair Portia:
The watery kingdom, whose ambitious head
Spits in the face of heaven, is no bar
To stop the foreign spirits; but they come,
As o'er a brook, to see fair Portia.
One of these three contains her heavenly picture.
Is't like that lead contains her? 'Twere damnation
To think so base a thought: it were too gross
To rib her cerecloth in the obscure grave.
Or shall I think in silver she's immured,
Being ten times undervalued to tried gold?
O sinful thought! Never so rich a gem
Was set in worse than gold. They have in England
A coin that bears the figure of an angel
Stamped in gold,—but that's insculpt upon;
But here an angel in a golden bed
Lies all within. —Deliver me the key:
Here do I choose, and thrive I as I may!

PORTIA.

There, take it, prince; and if my form lie there,
Then I am yours. [*He opens the golden casket*.

PRINCE OF MOROCCO.

O hell! what have we here?
A carrion Death, within whose empty eye
There is a written scroll! I'll read the writing.
All that glisters is not gold,—
Often have you heard that told:
Many a man his life hath sold
But my outside to behold:

40 **mortal-breathing**：breathing like a mortal.

41 **Hyrcanian**：of Hyrcania（里海之南老虎出没的荒野）。 **vasty**：vast. **wilds**：wilderness.

42 **throughfares**：thoroughfares.

43 **come view**：come to look at.

44 **watery kingdom**：ocean. **ambitious head**：stormy waves.

45 **bar**：barrier.

46 **spirits**：spirited persons.

49 **like**：likely. **'Twere**：it would be.

50 **were**：would be. **gross**：crude，粗陋，不恭敬。

51 **rib** (v.)：enclose with a strong protection，as with ribs. **cerecloth**['siəklɔθ]：waxed cloth，as winding-sheet（欧洲贵族旧俗用蜡布裹尸，用铅做棺材）。 **obscure**：hidden，dark.

52 **immured**[i'mjuəd]：enclosed，walled in.

53 **tried**：tempered，炼纯的。**Being…gold**：Silver was then one-tenth the value of gold. **to**：in comparison with.

56 **angel**：天使金币（一面刻有 St. Michael 天使刺杀毒龙的像，值十先令）。

57 **insculpt**：engraved. **upon**(adv.)：on the surface.

58 **an angel**：Portia's portrait.

60 **thrive I**：May I succeed.

63 **carrion**：rotten. **carrion Death**：death's head，skulk，骷髅。

64 **scroll**：纸卷。

65 **glisters**：glistens，发出金光。 **All…gold**：为部分否定句 = Not all that glisters is gold.

67 **sold**：出卖，丧失。

68 Only in order to see my outward appearance.

Gilded tombs do worms infold.
Had you been as wise as bold,
Young in limbs, in judgement old,
Your answer had not been inscroll'd:
Fare you well; your suit is cold.
Cold, indeed; and labour lost:
Then, farewell, heat; and welcome, frost! —
Portia, adieu. I have too grieved a heart
To take a tedious leave: thus losers part.
[*Exit with his* TRAIN. *Cornets*.

PORTIA.
A gentle riddance.—Draw the curtains, go.—
Let all of his complexion choose me so. [*Exeunt*.

SCENE VIII

Venice. A street.

Enter SALARINO *and* SOLANIO.

SALARINO.
Why, man, I saw Bassanio under sail:
With him is Gratiano gone along;
And in their ship I am sure Lorenzo is not.

SOLANIO.
The villain Jew with outcries raised the duke;
Who went with him to search Bassanio's ship.

SALARINO.
He came too late, the ship was under sail:
But there the duke was given to understand
That in a gondola were seen together
Lorenzo and his amorous Jessica:
Besides, Antonio certified the duke
They were not with Bassanio in his ship.

SOLANIO.

69 **infold**：enfold，enclose.

71 （As） young in limbs，（so） in judgement old.

72 **had not been**：would not have been. **inscroll'd**：written on this scroll.

73 **suit**：求婚。 **cold**：without power to move or influence.

75 **heat**：love（摩洛哥亲王已发誓，如失败则不再谈婚姻，见 II. i 40—43 行）。

77 **part**：depart.

78 **A gentle riddance**：走得知趣。

79 **his complexion**：① his like；②his skin color.

II.iii

4 **raised**：roused up.

7 **was given to understand**：was told.

8 **gondola** [ˈgɔndələ]：威尼斯的狭长的平底船，两头尖而翘起。

9 **amorous** [ˈæmərəs]：多情的。

10 **certified**：assured.

I never heard a passion so confused,
So strange, outrageous, and so variable,
As the dog Jew did utter in the streets:
'My daughter! —O my ducats! —O my daughter!
Fled with a Christian! —O my Christian ducats! —
Justice! the law! my ducats, and my daughter!
A sealed bag, two sealed bags of ducats,
Of double ducats, stol'n from me by my daughter!
And jewels, —two stones, two rich and precious stones,
Stol'n by my daughter! —Justice! find the girl!
She hath the stones upon her, and the ducats!'

SALARINO.

Why, all the boys in Venice follow him,
Crying,—his stones, his daughter, and his ducats.

SOLANIO.

Let good Antonio look he keep his day,
Or he shall pay for this.

SALARINO.

Marry, well remember'd,
I reason'd with a Frenchman yesterday,
Who told me, —in the narrow seas that part
The French and English, there miscarried
A vessel of our country richly fraught:
I thought upon Antonio when he told me;
And wisht in silence that it were not his.

SOLANIO.

You were best to tell Antonio what you hear;
Yet do not suddenly, for it may grieve him.

SALARINO.

A kinder gentleman treads not the earth.
I saw Bassanio and Antonio part:
Bassanio told him he would make some speed
Of his return: he answer'd, 'Do not so,—
Slubber not business for my sake, Bassanio,

12 **passion**: passionate outburst.

19 **double ducats**: ducats worth twice the value of the usual ones.

25 **look**: take care. **keep his day**: repays the money he owes by the appointed day，如期还钱。 **keep**:为假设语气。

26 **well remember'd**: You are right to remind me.

27 **reason'd**: talked.

28 **the narrow seas**: the English Channel.

29 **miscarried**: came to destruction, sank.

30 **fraught**: freighted, laden with goods.

33 **You were best**: it would be best for you.

39 **Slubber**: perform carelessly, do slovenly.

But stay the very riping of the time;
And for the Jew's bond which he hath of me,
Let it not enter in your mind of love:
Be merry; and employ your chiefest thoughts
To courtship, and such fair ostents of love
As shall conveniently become you there:'
And even there, his eye being big with tears,
Turning his face, he put his hand behind him,
And with affection wondrous sensible
He wrung Bassanio's hand; and so they parted.

SOLANIO.

I think he only loves the world for him.
I pray thee, let us go and find him out,
And quicken his embraced heaviness
With some delight or other.

SALARINO.

Do we so. [*Exeunt.*]

SCENE IX

Belmont. A room in PORTIA'S *house.*

Enter NERISSA *and a* SERVITOR.

NERISSA.

Quick, quick, I pray thee; draw the curtain straight:
The Prince of Arragon hath ta'en his oath,
And comes to his election presently.

Enter PRINCE OF ARRAGON, *his* TRAIN, *and* PORTIA.
Flourish of cornets.

PORTIA.

Behold, there stand the caskets, noble prince:
If you choose that wherein I am contain'd,
Straight shall our nuptial rites be solemnized:
But if you fail, without more speech, my lord,
You must be gone from hence immediately.

40 **stay**：wait for.

41 **for**：as regards.

42 **in**：into. **mind of love**：mind filled with love.

44 **ostents**：appearances.参见 II. ii 195 行。

45 **conveniently**：suitable. **become**：be fit.

48 **affection**：emotion. **wondrous**(adv.)：wonderfully，amazingly. **sensible**：intense.

52 **quicken**：enliven，stimulate. **embraced**：cherished，selfimposed. **heaviness**：sadness.

II.ix

1 **straight**：straightway，at once.

3 **election**：choice. **presently**：at once.

8 **from hence**：from here.

PRINCE OF ARRAGON.

I am enjoin'd by oath to observe three things:—
First, never to unfold to any one
Which casket 'twas I chose; next, if I fail
Of the right casket, never in my life
To woo a maid in way of marriage lastly,
If I do fail in fortune of my choice,
Immediately to leave you and be gone.

PORTIA.

To these injunctions every one doth swear
That comes to hazard for my worthless self.

PRINCE OF ARRAGON.

And so have I addrest me. Fortune now
To my heart's hope! —Gold, silver, and base lead.
'Who chooseth me must give and hazard all he hath.'
You shall look fairer, ere I give or hazard.
What says the golden chest? ha! let me see:
'Who chooseth me shall gain what many men desire.'
What many men desire! —that many may be meant
By the fool multitude, that choose by show,
Not learning more than the fond eye doth teach;
Which pries not to th' interior, but, like the martlet,
Builds in the weather on the outward wall,
Even in the force and road of casualty.
I will not choose what many men desire,
Because I will not jump with common spirits,
And rank me with the barbarous multitudes.
Why, then to thee, thou silver treasure-house;
Tell me once more what title thou dost bear:
'Who chooseth me shall get as much as he deserves:'
And well said too; for who shall go about
To cozen fortune, and be honourable
Without the stamp of merit? Let none presume
To wear an undeserved dignity.

9 **enjoin'd**：bound，obliged，受约束。

10 **unfold**：reveal，泄露。

13 **in way of**：in the way of.

15 **fortune**：luck.

17 **injunctions**：obligations，impositions.

19 **addrest me**：prepared myself.

22 **You**：指铅盒。

26 **By**：to refer to. **fool**：用作形容词 foolish.

27 **fond**：foolish.

28 **martlet**：European martin，欧洲燕子。

29 **in the weather**：in the open air.

30 **in the force and road of**：估计为拉丁语 in vi et via 的译文，意思 exposed to the attack of.

32 **jump with**：agree with. **common spirits**：ordinary persons.

33 **me**：myself.

35 **title**：inscription，motto.

38 **cozen**[ˈkʌzən]：cheat.

39 **stamp**：mark，character.

O, that estates, degrees, and offices,
Were not derived corruptly! and that clear honour
Were purchased by the merit of the wearer!
How many then should cover that stand bare!
How many be commanded that command!
How much low peasantry would then be glean'd
From the true seed of honour! and how much honour
Pickt from the chaff and ruin of the times,
To be new-varnisht! Well, but to my choice:
'Who chooseth me shall get as much as he deserves.'
I will assume desert.—Give me a key for this,
And instantly unlock my fortunes here.

[*He opens the silver casket*

PORTIA [*aside*].

Too long a pause for that which you find here.

PRINCE OF ARRAGON.

What's here? the portrait of a blinking idiot,
Presenting me a schedule! I will read it.
How much unlike art thou to Portia!
How much unlike my hopes and my deservings!
'Who chooseth me shall have as much as he deserves.'
Did I deserve no more than a fool's head?
Is that my prize? are my deserts no better?

PORTIA.

To offend, and judge, are distinct offices,
And of opposed natures.

PRINCE OF ARRAGON.

What is here?

The fire seven times tried this:
Seven times tried that judgement is,
That did never choose amiss.
Some there be that shadows kiss;
Such have but a shadow's bliss.
There be fools alive, Iwis,

41 **O, that**: O, how I wish that.

42 **derived**: gained, obtained. **clear**: unspotted,没有污点的。

43 **purchased**: gained, acquired.

44 **cover**: wear their hats (as equals). **bare**: bare-headed.

49 **new-varnished**: freshly painted(转义 invested with glory). **to my choice**: let me go to (or make) my choice.

51 **assume**: claim. **desert**[di'zəːt]: that which is due to me, 分内应得之物。

54 **blinking**: bloody (骂人的话)。

55 **schedule**: scroll with writing.

59 **fool's head**: 小丑画像。

60 **deserts**: merits.

61—62 作案和审判是截然相反的两件事,意味着你自己挑错了,不能仍由你来评判。

63 **tried**: tempered, refined.

65 **That**: which.

68 **Iwis**: (古英语 y-wiss) I know.

Silver'd o'er; and so was this.
Take what wife you will to bed,
I will ever be your head:
So be gone; you are sped.
Still more fool I shall appear
By the time I linger here:
With one fool's head I came to woo,
But I go away with two.—
Sweet, adieu. I'll keep my oath,
Patiently to bear my wroth.

[*Exit with his* TRAIN.

PORTIA.

Thus hath the candle singed the moth.
O, these deliberate fools! when they do choose,
They have the wisdom by their wit to lose.

NERISSA.

The ancient saying is no heresy,—
Hanging and wiving goes by destiny.

PORTIA.

Come, draw the curtain, Nerissa.

Enter a SERVANT.

SERVANT.

Where is my lady?

PORTIA.

Here: what would my lord?

SERVANT.

Madam, there is alighted at your gate
A young Venetian, one that comes before
To signify th' approaching of his lord;
From whom he bringeth sensible regreets,
To wit, besides commends and courteous breath,
Gifts of rich value. Yet I have not seen
So likely an ambassador of love:
A day in April never came so sweet,

69 **Silver'd o'er**:(who are) silver-plated,镀了银。 **this**: this casket.

70 **Take…bed**: No matter what wife you will take to bed.

71 **I…head**: you will always be a fool.

72 **sped**: despatched, done for.

74 **By the time**: the longer.

78 **wroth**: ruth, calamity.

81 **wit**: wisdom.

82 **heresy**['herəsi]:邪说。

83 两个抽象名词作主语,动词仍用单数。

85 **my lord**: Portia mocks the servant's high style.

89 **sensible regreets**: sincere greetings.

90 **To wit**: that is. **commends**: regards,问候。 **breath**: speech.

91 **Yet**:按现在词序在 not 之后,但过去可提前。

92 **likely**: handsome.

To show how costly summer was at hand,
As this fore-spurrer comes before his lord.

PORTIA.

No more, I pray thee: I am half afeard
Thou wilt say anon he is some kin to thee,
Thou spend'st such high-day wit in praising him.—
Come, come, Nerissa; for I long to see
Quick Cupid's post that comes so mannerly.

NERISSA.

Bassanio, lord Love, if thy will it be! [*Exeunt*.

94 **costly**: lavish, rich.

95 **fore-spurrer**: advance rider.

96 **afeard**: afraid.

97 **anon**: soon. **kin**: relative.

98 **high-day wit**: wit befitting a holiday.

100 **Quick**(adv.):修饰 see. **post**: messenger. **mannerly**: decently, civilly, 体面地。

101 **lord Love**: Cupid. **if thy will it be**: if it is your will.

ACT III

SCENE I

Venice. A street.

Enter SOLANIO *and* SALARINO.

SOLANIO.

Now, what news on the Rialto?

SOLANIO.

Why, yet it lives there uncheckt, that Antonio hath a ship of rich lading wrackt on the narrow seas; the Goodwins, I think they call the place; a very dangerous flat and fatal, where the carcasses of many a tall ship lie buried, as they say, if my gossip Report be an honest woman of her word.

SOLANIO.

I would she were as lying a gossip in that as ever knapt ginger, or made her neighbours believe she wept for the death of a third husband. But it is true, — without any slips of prolixity, or crossing the plain highway of talk, — that the good Antonio, the honest Antonio, —O, that I had a title good enough to keep his name company! —

SALARINO.

Come, the full stop.

SOLANIO.

Ha, — what sayest thou? —Why, the end is, he hath lost a ship.

SALARINO.

I would it might prove the end of his losses.

SOLANIO.

III.i

3 **it**：代替 that 引导的主语从句，而这里有 rumour 之义。**lives**：goes. **yet…uncheckt**：for the present the rumour circulates there without being challenged.

4—5 **of rich lading**：loaded with rich freight，载了贵重货品的。**wrackt**：wrecked. **the Goodwins**：the narrow seas，the English Channel.the Goodwin Sands，a dangerous shoal in the English Channel.

6 **flat**：shallow，shoal. **carcasses**：skeletons，remains.

7 **gossip**：饶舌妇。 **Report**：Rumour(拟人化)。

8 **of**：as regards.

9 **would**：wish. **she**：指 Report. **in that**：in that rumour.

10 **knapt**：chewed.

12—13 **slips**：slips of tongue. **prolixity**：too much talk. **without…prolixity**：毋庸赘言。 **plain highway of talk**：highway of plain speech. **crossing…talk**：横过直言不讳的康庄大道，即打叉。

16 **Come**：(表示不耐烦的感叹词)得啦。 **the full stop**：put the full stop to your remark.

Let me say amen betimes, lest the devil cross my prayer, — for here he comes in the likeness of a Jew.

Enter SHYLOCK.

How now, Shylock! what news among the merchants?

SHYLOCK.

You knew, none so well, none so well as you, of my daughter's flight.

SALARINO.

That's certain: I, for my part, knew the tailor that made the wings she flew withal.

SOLANIO.

And Shylock, for his own part, knew the bird was fledged; and then it is the complexion of them all to leave the dam.

SHYLOCK.

She is damn'd for it.

SALARINO.

That's certain, if the devil may be her judge.

SHYLOCK.

My own flesh and blood to rebel!

SOLANIO.

Out upon it, old carrion! rebels it at these years?

SHYLOCK.

I say my daughter is my flesh and blood.

SALARINO.

There is more difference between thy flesh and hers than between jet and ivory; more between your bloods than there is between red wine and rhenish. — But tell us, do you hear whether Antonio have had any loss at sea or no?

SHYLOCK.

There I have another bad match: a bankrout, a prodigal, who dare scarce show his head on the Rialto; — a beggar, that was used to come so smug upon the

20 **betimes**: in good time. **cross**: intercept.

23 **none so well**: nobody else knew so well.

26 **withal**: with.

28 **fledged**: fit to fly. **complexion**: nature, disposition.

29 **dam**: dame, mother (of animal or bird).

30 **She**: Jessica.

33 **Out upon it**: 呸!(表示愤怒或憎恶的感叹语) **carrion**: term of contempt for a living person, as being no better than carrion. **it**: 代前面的 flesh and blood. Solanio 故意误解 Shylock 的话,用 flesh and blood 来指 Shylock 的血性和肉欲。

36 **jet**: 黑色大理石,煤玉。

37 **rhenish**: 莱茵河流域的白葡萄酒,当时被认为是上等酒。

40 **match**: bargain. **bankrout**: bankrupt person.

41 **show his head**: make his appearance.

42 **that**: who 在当时关系代词 that 可用于非限制性定语从句。**used**: accustomed. **smug**: neatly dressed.

mart; — let him look to his bond; he was wont to call me usurer; — let him look to his bond: he was wont to lend money for a Christian courtesy: — let him look to his bond.

SALARINO.

Why, I am sure, if he forfeit, thou wilt not take his flesh: what's that good for?

SHYLOCK.

To bait fish withal: if it will feed nothing else, it will feed my revenge. He hath disgraced me, and hinder'd me half a million; laught at my losses, mockt at my gains, scorn'd my nation, thwarted my bargains, cooled my friends, heated mine enemies: and what's his reason? I am a Jew. Hath not a Jew eyes? hath not a Jew hands, organs, dimensions, senses, affections, passions? fed with the same food, hurt with the same weapons, subject to the same diseases, heal'd by the same means, warm'd and cool'd by the same winter and summer, as a Christian is? If you prick us, do we not bleed? if you tickle us, do we not laugh? if you poison us, do we not die? and if you wrong us, shall we not revenge? if we are like you in the rest, we will resemble you in that. If a Jew wrong a Christian, what is his humility? revenge: if a Christian wrong a Jew, what should his sufferance be by Christian example? why, revenge. The villainy you teach me, I will execute; and it shall go hard but I will better the instruction.

Enter a SERVANT *from* ANTONIO.

SERVANT.

Gentlemen, my master Antonio is at his house, and desires to speak with you both.

SALARINO.

We have been up and down to seek him.

43 mart：market place.

45 for a Christian courtesy：as an act of Christian kindness，i.e. without taking interest.

47 forfeit：fails to keep his obligation.

50—51 hinder'd me half a million：me 后面省略介词 from，等于说 prevented me from making a half-million profit.

65—66 sufferance：bearing with patience，耐心忍受。

67—68 it shall go hard but I will better the instruction：it will be my fault if I do not improve on the lesson.

71 up and down：to every place，到处。

SOLANIO.

Here comes another of the tribe: a third cannot be matcht, unless the devil himself turn Jew.

[*Exeunt* SOLANIO, SALARINO, *and* SERVANT.

Enter TUBAL.

SHYLOCK.

How now, Tubal! what news from Genoa? hast thou found my daughter?

TUBAL.

I often came where I did hear of her, but cannot find her.

SHYLOCK.

Why, there, there, there, there! a diamond gone, cost me two thousand ducats in Frankfort! The curse never fell upon our nation till now; I never felt if till now: — two thousand ducats in that; and other precious, precious jewels. — I would my daughter were dead at my foot, and the jewels in her ear! would she were hearsed at my foot, and the ducats in her coffin! No news of them? — Why, so: — and I know not what's spent in the search: why, thou, loss upon loss! the thief gone with so much, and so much to find the thief; and no satisfaction, no revenge: nor no ill luck stirring but what lights on my shoulders; no sighs but of my breathing; no tears but of my shedding.

TUBAL.

Yes, other men have ill luck too: Antonio, as I heard in Genoa,—

SHYLOCK.

What, what, what? ill luck, ill luck?

TUBAL.

Hath an argosy cast away, coming from Tripolis.

SHYLOCK.

77 there!：感叹词。 **cost**：it cost.

78 Frankfort：German city Frankfurt，famous for its fairs，at which fine jewelry was sold.

81 would：wish.

83 hearsed：on her bier.

88 but what lights on：that does not fall on.

89 but：that are not.

91 Yes：否定前面的否定句，英语用"yes".

94 cast away：wrecked，sank，沉没。

I thank God, I thank God! —Is't true, is't true?

TUBAL.

I spoke with some of the sailors that escaped the wrack.

SHYLOCK.

I thank thee, good Tubal: —good news, good news! ha, ha! —where? in Genoa?

TUBAL.

Your daughter spent in Genoa, as I heard, one night fourscore ducats.

SHYLOCK.

Thou stick'st a dagger in me: — I shall never see my gold again: fourscore ducats at a sitting! fourscore ducats!

TUBAL.

There came divers of Antonio's creditors in my company to Venice, that swear he cannot choose but break.

SHYLOCK.

I am very glad of it: — I'll plague him; I'll torture him: —I am glad on't.

TUBAL.

One of them show'd me a ring that he had of your daughter for a monkey.

SHYLOCK.

Out upon her! Thou torturest me, Tubal: it was my turquoise; I had it of Leah when I was a bachelor: I would not have given it for a wilderness of monkeys.

TUBAL.

But Antonio is certainly undone.

SHYLOCK.

Nay, that's true, that's very true. Go, Tubal, fee me an officer; bespeak him a fortnight before. I will have the heart of him, if he forfeit; for, were he out of Venice, I can make what merchandise I will.

96 **escaped**：后面省略介词 from.

104 **divers**：various.

106 **break**：go bankrupt.

108 **on't**：of it.

109 **had of**：got from.

111 **Out upon her!**：Damn her!

112 **turquoise**：绿松石。 **Leah**[liə]：Shylock's wife.

113 **a wilderness of monkeys**：漫山遍野的猴子。

114 **undone**：ruined，done for.

115 **Nay**：可不是(在这里等于 yes). **fee me**：engage for me.

116 **officer**：sergeant of the law who made arrests for debt. **bespeak**：engage，预先雇好。

118 **merchandise**：bargain，traffic.

Go, Tubal, and meet me at our synagogue; go, good
Tubal; at our synagogue, Tubal. [*Exeunt*.

SCENE II

Belmont. A room in PORTIA'S *house*.

Enter BASSANIO, PORTIA, GRATIANO, NERISSA, *and all their* TRAIN.

PORTIA.

I pray you, tarry: pause a day or two
Before you hazard; for, in choosing wrong,
I lose your company: therefore, forbear awhile.
There's something tells me—but it is not love—
I would not lose you; and you know yourself,
Hate counsels not in such a quality.
But lest you should not understand me well,—
And yet a maiden hath no tongue but thought,—
I would detain you here some month or two
Before you venture for me. I could teach you
How to choose right, but then I am forsworn;
So will I never be: so may you miss me;
But if you do, you'll make me wish a sin,
That I had been forsworn. Beshrew your eyes,
They have o'erlookt me, and divided me;
One half of me is yours, the other half yours,—
Mine own, I would say; but if mine, then yours,
And so all yours! O, these naughty times
Put bars between the owners and their rights!
And so, though yours, not yours. —Prove it so,
Let fortune go to hell for it, —not I.
I speak too long; but 'tis to peize the time,
To eke it, and to draw it out in length,
To stay you from election.

BASSANIO.

119 synagogue：犹太教教堂。

III.ii

2 in choosing wrong：in the event of your choosing wrong.

3 forbear：abstain from doing something. **awhile**：a while，some time.

4 tells：前省略 which.

5 would not：shall not.

6 quality：manner.

8 a maiden hath no tongue but thought：a maiden should not speak out everything she thinks.

11 then I am forsworn：if I do so，I shall renounce what I swore.

12 miss：选不中。

14 Beshrew：curse，the Devil take（温和咒语）。

15 o'erlookt：bewitched.

18 naughty：bad，wicked.

20 Prove it so：If it is proved to be so.

22 peize（由法语 peser 而来）：retard by hanging weights.

23 eke：increase. **draw…length**：lengthen.

24 stay：keep. **election**：choosing.

Let me choose;
For, as I am, I live upon the rack.

PORTIA.

Upon the rack, Bassanio! then confess
What treason there is mingled with your love.

BASSANIO.

None but that ugly treason of mistrust,
Which makes me fear the enjoying of my love:
There may as well be amity and league
'Tween snow and fire, as treason and my love.

PORTIA.

Ay, but I fear you speak upon the rack,
Where men enforced do speak any thing.

BASSANIO.

Promise me life, and I'll confess the truth.

PORTIA.

Well then, confess, and live.

BASSANIO.

'Confess,' and 'love,'
Had been the very sum of my confession:
O happy torment, when my torturer
Doth teach me answers for deliverance!
But let me to my fortune and the caskets.

PORTIA.

Away, then! I am lockt in one of them:
If you do love me, you will find me out.—
Nerissa, and the rest, stand all aloof.—
Let music sound while he doth make his choice;
Then, if he lose, he makes a swan-like end,
Fading in music: that the comparison
May stand more proper, my eye shall be the stream
And watery death-bed for him. He may win;
And what is music then? then music is
Even as the flourish when true subjects bow

25 **as I am**：in my present condition. **rack**：torture rack.

29 **fear**：后面省略介词 for.

30 **amity**：friendship. **league**：agreement，unity.

31 **'Tween**：between.

33 **enforced**：under compulsion.

36 **Had been**：would have been.

40 **I**：my image.

42 **aloof**：at a distance (so as not to interfere).

44 **makes…end**：swans break into song for the first and only time before dying.

45 **Fading**：dying. **that**：in order that.

46 **eye**：eye filled with tears.

49 **as**：like. **flourish**：a sounding of trumpets.

To a new-crowned monarch: such it is
As are those dulcet sounds in break of day
That creep into the dreaming bridegroom's ear,
And summon him to marriage.—Now he goes,
With no less presence, but with much more love,
Than young Alcides, when he did redeem
The virgin tribute paid by howling Troy
To the sea-monster: I stand for sacrifice;
The rest aloof are the Dardanian wives,
With bleared visages, come forth to view
The issue of th' exploit. Go, Hercules!
Live thou, I live: —with much much more dismay
I view the fight than thou that makest the fray.

Here music.—A Song, the whilst BASSANIO *comments on the caskets to himself.*

Tell me where is fancy bred,
Or in the heart or in the head?
How begot, how nourished?
Reply, reply.
It is engender'd in the eyes,
With gazing fed; and fancy dies
In the cradle where it lies.
Let us all ring fancy's knell;
I'll begin it,—Ding, dong, bell.
All. Ding, dong, bell.

BASSANIO.

So may the outward shows be least themselves:
The world is still deceived with ornament.
In law, what plea so tainted and corrupt,
But, being season'd with a gracious voice,
Obscures the show of evil? In religion,
What damned error, but some sober brow
Will bless it, and approve it with a text,
Hiding the grossness with fair ornament?

51 **dulcet**：sweet. **dulcet sounds**：an allusion to the custom of playing music under the bridegroom's window on the morning of his marriage.

54 **presence**：dignity of manner.

55 **Alcides**[æl'saidiːz]：希腊神话中的大力英雄，即 Hercules，他从海怪那里救出特洛伊公主 Hesione，即第 56 行所说的 virgin tribute.

56 **howling**：lamenting.

57 **I…sacrifice**：I stand here instead of Hesione for sacrifice.

58 **Dardanian**：Trojan.

59 **bleared visages**：tear-stained faces. **come**：who have come.

60 **issue**：outcome，result. **exploit**：heroic deed.

61 **Live thou**：should you live.

62 **fray**：single combat.

the whilst：while.

63—64 **fancy**：love. **bred,head**：都同 lead 押韵，内容则说只凭外表的爱情很快夭折，Portia 叫唱这支歌，颇有暗示性。 **Or … or**：whether … or.

65 **begot**(p.p.)：begotten. **nourished**(p.p.)：fed.

67 **engender'd**：born.

69 **cradle**：指 eyes.

73 **least**：of least value.

74 **still**：always. **with**：by.

75 **plea**：辩词。 **tainted**：evil-tasting.

76 **But**(关系代词)：that … not. **season'd**：spiced，变质的肉加以香料使味道变好。 **gracious**：attractive，beautiful 动听的。

78 **damned**：遭天谴的。 **sober**：serious，grave. **brow**：forehead，the whole countenance（这里指道貌岸然的人，是用部分代整体的一种提喻 synecdoche）.

79 **approve**：commend. **text**：a passage from the Bible.

80 **grossness**：shocking offence.

There is no vice so simple, but assumes
Some mark of virtue on his outward parts:
How many cowards, whose hearts are all as false
As stairs of sand, wear yet upon their chins
The beards of Hercules and frowning Mars;
Who, inward searcht, have livers white as milk;
And these assume but valour's excrement
To render them redoubted! Look on beauty,
And you shall see 'tis purchased by the weight;
Which therein works a miracle in nature,
Making them lightest that wear most of it:
So are those crisped snaky golden locks,
Which make such wanton gambols with the wind,
Upon supposed fairness, often known
To be the dowry of a second head,
The skull that bred them in the sepulchre.
Thus ornament is but the guiled shore
To a most dangerous sea; the beauteous scarf
Veiling an Indian beauty; in a word,
The seeming truth which cunning times put on
To entrap the wisest. Therefore, thou gaudy gold,
Hard food for Midas, I will none of thee;
Nor none of thee, thou stale and common drudge
'Tween man and man: but thou, thou meagre lead,
Which rather threatenest than dost promise aught,
Thy paleness moves me more than eloquence;
And here choose I: —joy be the consequence!

PORTIA [*aside*].

How all the other passions fleet to air,—
As doubtful thoughts, and rash-embraced despair,
And shuddering fear, and green-eyed jealousy!
O love, be moderate; allay thy ecstasy;
In measure rain thy joy; scant this excess!
I feel too much thy blessing: make it less,

81 **vice**：拟人化则指坏人(莎士比亚剧本中常有这种用抽象名词指人的转喻用法)。 **but assumes**：that does not put on.

82 **his**：its. **parts**：features.

85 **frowning**：stern-looking,容颜严峻的。 **Mars**：罗马神话中的战神。

86 **have…milk**：are white-livered(cowardly).

87 **but**：merely. **excrement**['ekskrimənt]：outward growth, like hair and beard. **valour's excrement**：a soldier's beard (Beards are a sign of virility and bravery).

88 **redoubted**：redoubtable, formidable,令人生畏的。

89 **'tis…weight**：美貌(化妆品)可以论斤两用钱买到。

91 **lightest**：双关语 1.最轻；2.最轻狂,最不贞洁。

92—96 **crisped**：curled. **supposed fairness**：假的白净。 **dowry**：possession. **the…head**：wig. **crisped…sepulchre**：curly golden hair is often a wig, made from the hair of a corpse. **them**：指 locks, 后面省略 being.

97 **guiled**：guileful, treacherous.

99 **Indian**：dark, which was then not considered beautiful by the Europeans.

102 **Midas**：king of Phrygia,他求神使他的手指能把任何东西点化成金,结果食物也变成不可食的黄金。 **I will none**：I will have none.

103 **drudge**：servant (of exchange and commerce),指银子。

104 **meagre**：poor, barren.

108 **fleet to air**：fly away.

109 **As**：namely. **rash-embraced**：rashly-entertained.

110 **green-eyed jealousy**：绿色常被用来修饰嫉妒。

112 **In measure**：moderately,适度地。 **scant**(v.t.)：make less.

113 **thy**：指 love's.

For fear I surfeit!

BASSANIO.

What find I here?

[*Opening the leaden casket.*

Fair Portia's counterfeit! What demi-god
Hath come so near creation? Move these eyes?
Or whether, riding on the balls of mine,
Seem they in motion? Here are sever'd lips,
Parted with sugar breath: so sweet a bar
Should sunder such sweet friends. Here in her hairs
The painter plays the spider; and hath woven
A golden mesh t'entrap the hearts of men,
Faster than gnats in cobwebs: but her eyes,—
How could he see to do them? having made one,
Methinks it should have power to steal both his,
And leave itself unfurnisht. Yet look, how far
The substance of my praise doth wrong this shadow
In underprizing it, so far this shadow
Doth limp behind the substance.—Here's the scroll,
The continent and summary of my fortune.

You that choose not by the view,
Chance as fair, and choose as true!
Since this fortune falls to you,
Be content, and seek no new.
If you be well pleased with this,
And hold your fortune for your bliss,
Turn you where your lady is,
And claim her with a loving kiss.

A gentle scroll.—Fair lady, by your leave; [*Kissing her.*
I come by note, to give and to receive.
Like one of two contending in a prize,
That thinks he hath done well in people's eyes,
Hearing applause and universal shout,
Giddy in spirit, still gazing in a doubt

114 **surfeit**: have too much.

116 **counterfeit**: portrait. **demi-god**: half-god (referring to the portraitist).

118 **Or whether**: or. **balls**: eye-balls.

119 **sever'd**: parted.

120 **bar**: anything that seperates, here referring to "breath".

121 **sunder**: separate. **friends**: i.e., lips.

124 **Faster**: firmer, tighter. **than … cobwebs**: than gnats are entrapped in cobwebs.

125 **he**: the artist. **do**: paint.

126 **Methinks**: I think. **steal both his**: blind both his eyes.

127 **unfurnisht**: unmatched with its fellow. **how**: as.

128 **shadow**: portrait.

129 **underprizing**: undervaiuing.

130 **substance**: 指 Portia 本人。

131 **continent**: sum.

133 **Chance**(v.i.): meet with a fortune. **true**(adv.): right.

137 **hold … for**: regard … as.

139 **claim**: demand as a right.

140 **by your leave**: with your permission.

141 **by note**: by a bill of dues.

143 **That**: who.

Whether those peals of praise be his or no;
So, thrice-fair lady, stand I, even so;
As doubtful whether what I see be true,
Until confirm'd, sign'd, ratified by you.

PORTIA.

You see me, Lord Bassanio, where I stand,
Such as I am: though for myself alone
I would not be ambitious in my wish,
To wish myself much better; yet for you
I would be trebled twenty times myself;
A thousand times more fair, ten thousand times
More rich;
That, only to stand high in your account,
I might in virtues, beauties, livings, friends,
Exceed account: but the full sum of me
Is sum of nothing; which, to term in gross,
Is an unlesson'd girl, unschool'd, unpractised:
Happy in this, she is not yet so old
But she may learn; happier than this,
She is not bred so dull but she can learn;
Happiest of all is that her gentle spirit
Commits itself to yours to be directed,
As from her lord, her governor, her king.
Myself and what is mine to you and yours
Is now converted: but now I was the lord
Of this fair mansion, master of my servants,
Queen o'er myself; and even now, but now,
This house, these servants, and this same myself,
Are yours, my lord: I give them with this ring;
Which when you part from, lose, or give away,
Let it presage the ruin of your love,
And be my vantage to exclaim on you.

BASSANIO.

Madam, you have bereft me of all words,

157 **That**: so that. **account**: estimation, 评价。

158 **livings**: possessions, tenures.

159 **Exceed account**: be innumerable, 数不尽。

160 **term in gross**: mention in total, mention its full account.

161 **unlesson'd**: uneducated. **unpractised**: inexperienced.

162 **Happy in this**: She is fortunate in the fact that….

163 **But she can learn**: that she cannot learn.

165 **is**: 后面省略 it 或 this.

169 **converted**: transferred, 转给。 **but now**: just now, a moment ago.

171 **but now**: at the present moment.

175 **it**: 代上一行的从句。

176 **vantage**: opportunity. **exclaim on**: cry out against, reproach.

177 **bereft…words**: made me speechless.

Only my blood speaks to you in my veins:
And there is such confusion in my powers,
As, after some oration fairly spoke
By a beloved prince, there doth appear
Among the buzzing pleased multitude;
Where every something, being blent together,
Turns to a wild of nothing, save of joy,
Exprest and not exprest. But when this ring
Parts from this finger, then parts life from hence:
O, then be bold to say Bassanio's dead!

NERISSA.

My lord and lady, it is now our time,
That have stood by, and seen our wishes prosper,
To cry, good joy:—good joy, my lord and lady!

GRATIANO.

My Lord Bassanio and my gentle lady,
I wish you all the joy that you can wish;
For I am sure you can wish none from me:
And, when your honours mean to solemnize
The bargain of your faith, I do beseech you,
Even at that time I may be married too.

BASSANIO.

With all my heart, so thou canst get a wife.

GRATIANO.

I thank your lordship, you have got me one.
My eyes, my lord, can look as swift as yours:
You saw the mistress, I beheld the maid;
You loved, I loved; for intermission
No more pertains to me, my lord, than you.
Your fortune stood upon the caskets there;
And so did mine too, as the matter falls;
For wooing here, until I sweat again,
And swearing, till my very roof was dry
With oaths of love, at last,—if promise last,—

178 Only 的位置应在 in 之前,当时允许这种挪位。

179 **powers**: faculties.

180 **spoke**(p.p.): spoken. **As**: 关系代词,引导定语从句,as 在从句中作主语,其先行词为 confusion,其动词为 doth appear.

183 **something**: a certain thing, a certain quantity.

184 **wild of nothing**: chaos. **save**: except.

186 **from hence**: from here, from me.

189 **That**: who. **wishes**: 指希望 Bassanio 挑中彩盒的心愿。

190 **To cry**: 作定语修饰 time. **good joy**: We wish you good joy. 恭喜。

193 **none from me**: none differently from me, none which I do not wish you.

194 **your honours**: 对两个人的尊称,故用复数。

195 **bargain of your faith**: 你们立下誓言要做的事。

197 **so**: so long as, if only.

201 **intermission**: delay, cessation, 迟延,停止。

202 **pertains to**: belongs to.

203 **stood upon**: depended upon.

204 **as…falls**: as it happens.

205 **sweat**: sweated 因最后为 t 音而 ed 省略。 **again**: used to indicate intensity of action.

206 **roof**: roof of the mouth, palate.

207 **if promise last**: if her promise lasts (endures).

I got a promise of this fair one here,
To have her love, provided that your fortune
Achieved her mistress.

PORTIA.

Is this true, Nerissa?

NERISSA.

Madam, it is, so you stand pleased withal.

BASSANIO.

And do you, Gratiano, mean good faith?

GRATIANO.

Yes, faith, my lord.

BASSANIO.

Our feast shall be much honour'd in your marriage.

GRATIANO.

We'll play with them the first boy for a thousand ducats.

NERISSA.

What, and stake down?

GRATIANO.

No; we shall ne'er win at that sport, and stake down.—
But who comes here? Lorenzo and his infidel?
What, and my old Venetian friend Solanio?

Enter LORENZO, JESSICA, *and* SOLANIO.

BASSANIO.

Lorenzo and Solanio, welcome hither;
If that the youth of my new interest here
Have power to bid you welcome.—By your leave,
I bid my very friends and countrymen,
Sweet Portia, welcome.

PORTIA.

So do I, my lord;
They are entirely welcome.

LORENZO.

I thank your honour.—For my part, my lord,
My purpose was not to have seen you here;

208 **of**：from.

210 **Achieved**：should win.

211 **so**：provided that. **stand…withal**：is pleased with it.

213 **faith**：in faith，really.

215 **play**：wager.

216 **stake down**：lay down the stake.

217 **and stake down**：with stake down，如果阴茎倒下了。

218 **infidel**[ˈinfidəl]：异教徒。

221 **If that**：if. **youth**：short time. **new interest**：newly acquired right to possessions.

222 **Have**：subjunctive present. **By your leave**：with your permission (addressed to Portia).

223 **very**：veritable，true.

227 **to have seen**：完成体不定式，旧时比今天用得多。

But meeting with Solanio by the way,
He did entreat me, past all saying nay,
To come with him along.

SOLANIO.

I did, my lord;
And I have reason for't. Signior Antonio
Commends him to you. [*Gives* BASSANIO *a letter*.

BASSANIO.

Ere I ope his letter,
I pray you, tell me how my good friend doth.

SOLANIO.

Not sick, my lord, unless it be in mind;
Not well, unless in mind: his letter there
Will show you his estate. [BASSANIO *reads the letter*.

GRATIANO.

Nerissa, cheer yon stranger; bid her welcome.—
Your hand, Solanio: what's the news from Venice?
How doth that royal merchant, good Antonio?
I know he will be glad of our success;
We are the Jasons, we have won the fleece.

SOLANIO.

I would you had won the fleece that he hath lost!

PORTIA.

There are some shrewd contents in yon same paper,
That steals the colour from Bassanio's cheek:
Some dear friend dead; else nothing in the world
Could turn so much the constitution
Of any constant man. What, worse and worse! —
With leave, Bassanio; I am half yourself,
And I must freely have the half of any thing
That this same paper brings you.

BASSANIO.

O sweet Portia,
Here are a few of the unpleasant'st words

229 **past…nay**：admitting of no denial.

230 **along**：旧时常放在句末，现在应在 with 之前。

232 **him**：himself. **Commends…you**：向你致意。 **Ere**：before. **ope**：open.

235 **unless in mind**：unless he can get well in mind，除非心病好了。

236 **estate**：state，condition.

237 **yon**：yonder. **stranger**：alien 指 Jessica.

239 **doth**：fares. **royal**：powerful and wealthy as a king.

241 **Jasons**：见 I. i 171—172 行。

242 **fleece**：和 fleets 同音。

243 **shrewd**：bad，distressing.

246 **constitution**：frame of mind.

247 **constant**：steady，well-balanced.

248 **With leave**：with your permission.

249 **freely have the half of**：rightfully share.

That ever blotted paper! Gentle lady,
When I did first impart my love to you,
I freely told you, all the wealth I had
Ran in my veins,—I was a gentleman;
And then I told you true: and yet, dear lady,
Rating myself at nothing, you shall see
How much I was a braggart. When I told you
My state was nothing, I should then have told you
That I was worse than nothing; for, indeed,
I have engaged myself to a dear friend,
Engaged my friend to his mere enemy,
To feed my means. Here is a letter, lady,—
The paper as the body of my friend,
And every word in it a gaping wound,
Issuing life-blood.—But is it true, Solanio?
Have all his ventures fail'd? What, not one hit?
From Tripolis, from Mexico, and England,
From Lisbon, Barbary, and India?
And not one vessel scape the dreadful touch
Of merchant-marring rocks?

SOLANIO.

Not one, my lord.
Besides, it should appear, that if he had
The present money to discharge the Jew,
He would not take it. Never did I know
A creature, that did bear the shape of man,
So keen and greedy to confound a man;
He plies the duke at morning and at night;
And doth impeach the freedom of the state,
If they deny him justice: twenty merchants,
The duke himself, and the magnificoes
Of greatest port, have all persuaded with him;
But none can drive him from the envious plea
Of forfeiture, of justice, and his bond.

254—255 **freely**：frankly. **all … veins**，i.e. I was a penniless nobleman，except for gentle birth I had nothing.

255 **gentleman**：person born of a noble family.

257 **rating myself at nothing**：把自己估价为身无分文。

259 **My … nothing**：I was penniless.

261 **engaed … to**：pledged myself to，owed money to.

262 **Engaged … to**：bound（pledged）my friend to，caused my friend to be in debt to. **mere**：sheer，out-and-out.

263 **feed**：supply.

264 （独立主格结构）the paper being like the body of my friend.

267 **ventures**：things put to risk，here ships. **hit**：success.

269 **Barbary**：非洲西北部。

270 **scape**：escape(假设语气)。

271 **merchant-marring**：毁坏商船的。

272 **should**：would.

273 **present**：available. **discharge**：pay his debt to.

276 **confound**：ruin.

277 **plies**：assails（a person）with arguments and requests.注意当时可说 at morning.

278 **impeach**：call in question. **freedom**：franchise，right of citizens.

279 **deny him justice**：不给他依法办理。

280 **magnificoes**：highest nobles.

281 **port**：dignity. **persuaded with**：tried to persuade，argued with.

282 **envious**：malicious.

JESSICA.

When I was with him, I have heard him swear,
To Tubal and to Chus, his countrymen,
That he would rather have Antonio's flesh
Than twenty times the value of the sum
That he did owe him: and I know, my lord,
If law, authority, and power deny not,
It will go hard with poor Antonio.

PORTIA.

Is it your dear friend that is thus in trouble?

BASSANIO.

The dearest friend to me, the kindest man,
The best-condition'd and unwearied spirit
In doing courtesies; and one in whom
The ancient Roman honour more appears
Than any that draws breath in Italy.

PORTIA.

What sum owes he the Jew?

BASSANIO.

For me three thousand ducats.

PORTIA.

What, no more?
Pay him six thousand, and deface the bond;
Double six thousand, and then treble that,
Before a friend of this description
Shall lose a hair through Bassanio's fault.
First go with me to church and call me wife,
And then away to Venice to your friend;
For never shall you lie by Portia's side
With an unquiet soul. You shall have gold
To pay the petty debt twenty times over:
When it is paid, bring your true friend along.
My maid Nerissa and myself meantime
Will live as maids and widows. Come, away!

290 **go hard**：fare ill.

293 **best-condition'd**：kindest-hearted, of the best cast of mind，心地最好的。 **spirit**：person.

294 **courtesies**：acts of kindness.

299 **deface**：cancel.

303 **call me wife**：marry me.

For you shall hence upon your wedding-day:
Bid your friends welcome, show a merry cheer:
Since you are dear-bought, I will love you dear.—
But let me hear the letter of your friend.

BASSANIO [*reads*].

Sweet Bassanio, my ships have all miscarried, my creditors grow cruel, my estate is very low, my bond to the Jew is forfeit; and since in paying it, it is impossible I should live, all debts are clear'd between you and I, if I might but see you at my death. Notwithstanding, use your pleasure: if your love do not persuade you to come, let not my letter.

PORTIA.

O love, dispatch all business, and be gone!

BASSANIO.

Since I have your good leave to go away,
I Will make haste: but, till I come again,
No bed shall e'er be guilty of my stay,
No rest be interposer 'twixt us twain.

[*Exeunt*.

SCENE III

Venice. A street.

Enter SHYLOCK, SALARINO, ANTONIO, *and* GAOLER.

SHYLOCK.

Gaoler, look to him:—tell not me of mercy;—
This is the fool that lent out money gratis:—
Gaoler, look to him.

ANTONIO.

Hear me yet, good Shylock.

SHYLOCK.

I'll have my bond; speak not against my bond:

311 **shall hence**：shall leave here.

312 **cheer**：countenance，face.

315 **Sweet**：dear. **miscarried**：came to destruction.

316 **estate**：financial condition. **low**：poor.

317 **paying it**：it 指 bond.

318—319 **between you and I**：用 I 代替 me，是为了音调好听。

320 **use your pleasure**：do as you please.

322 **love**(n.)：亲爱的。 **dispatch**：finish，wind up.

323 **leave**：permission.

325 **No…stay**：I will not go to bed.

326 **'twixt**：between. **twain**：two.

III.iii

1 **Gaoler**[ˈdʒeilə]：jailer，狱卒，牢头。 **look to**：watch，看住。

2 **gratis**[ˈgreitis]：free of interest，不取利息。

4 **have my bond**：have my right according to the bond，得到借据给我的权利。

I have sworn an oath that I will have my bond.
Thou call'dst me dog before thou hadst a cause;
But, since I am a dog, beware my fangs:
The duke shall grant me justice.—I do wonder,
Thou naughty gaoler, that thou art so fond
To come abroad with him at his request.

ANTONIO.

I pray thee, hear me speak.

SHYLOCK.

I'll have my bond; I will not hear thee speak:
I'll have my bond; and therefore speak no more.
I'll not be made a soft and dull-eyed fool,
To shake the head, relent, and sigh, and yield
To Christian intercessors. Follow not;
I'll have no speaking: I will have my bond.[*Exit*.

SALARINO.

It is the most impenetrable cur
That ever kept with men.

ANTONIO.

Let him alone:
I'll follow him no more with bootless prayers.
He seeks my life; his reason well I know:
I oft deliver'd from his forfeitures
Many that have at times made moan to me;
Therefore he hates me.

SALARINO.

I am sure the duke
Will never grant this forfeiture to hold.

ANTONIO.

The duke cannot deny the course of law;
For the commodity that strangers have
With us in Venice, if it be denied,
Will much impeach the justice of the state;
Since that the trade and profit of the city

9 **naughty**：worthless，wicked. **fond**：foolish.

10 **To**：as to. **abroad**：out.

14 **dull-eyed**：wanting in perception.

15 **shake the head**：用 the 不用 my 是受法语的影响。

16 **intercessors**：those who plead or act in favour of others，为人说情者。

18 **impenetrable**：not to be moved.

19 **kept**：lived，resided.

20 **bootless**：useless. **prayers**：entreaties.

22 **oft**：often. **deliver'd**：set free，rescued. **forfeitures**：penalties for breach of contract.

23 **moan**：lamentation.

25 **grant**：allow. **hold**：hold good，be valid，有效。

27 **commodity**：convenience (in trade). **strangers**：foreigners.

29 **impeach**：discredit. **justice**：法治。

30 **Since that**：since.

Consisteth of all nations. Therefore, go:
These griefs and losses have so bated me,
That I shall hardly spare a pound of flesh
To-morrow to my bloody creditor.—
Well, gaoler, on.—Pray God, Bassanio come
To see me pay his debt,—and then I care not! [*Exeunt.*

SCENE IV

Belmont. A room in PORTIA'S *house.*

Enter PORTIA, NERISSA, LORENZO, JESSICA, *and* BALTHAZAR, *a man of* PORTIA'S.

LORENZO.

Madam, although I speak it in your presence,
You have a noble and a true conceit
Of god-like amity; which appears most strongly
In bearing thus the absence of your lord.
But if you knew to whom you show this honour,
How true a gentleman you send relief,
How dear a lover of my lord your husband,
I know you would be prouder of the work
Than customary bounty can enforce you.

PORTIA.

I never did repent for doing good,
Nor shall not now: for in companions
That do converse and waste the time together,
Whose souls do bear an egal yoke of love,
There must be needs a like proportion
Of lineaments, of manners, and of spirit;
Which makes me think that this Antonio,
Being the bosom lover of my lord,
Must needs be like my lord. If it be so,
How little is the cost I have bestow'd
In purchasing the semblance of my soul

31 Consisteth of：rely on.

32 bated：reduced，made thin.

33 spare：afford to give.

34 bloody：bloodthirsty.

35 on：go on，走吧。 **Bassanio come**：May Bassanio come.

III.iv

1—2 although… ,You…：although… ,I must say…虽然是当你的面，我也必须说，你……；不是我当面恭维，你……。

2 conceit：understanding.

3 amity：friendship. **which**：代 conceit.

6 relief：aid.

7 my lord：对 Bassanio 的尊称。

9 customary：ordinary，common. **bounty**：liberality，kindness. **enforce**：compel.

11 Nor shall not：nor shall.

12 That：who. **waste**：spend.

13 egal yoke：equal burden.

14 needs：of necessity. **like**：similar.

15 lineaments[ˈliniəmənts]：features，容貌。

17 lover：friend. **my lord**：my husband.

19 bestow'd：spent.

20 semblance of my soul：one who is like Bassanio，whom I love as my own soul.

From out the state of hellish cruelty!
This comes too near the praising of myself;
Therefore no more of it: hear other things.—
Lorenzo, I commit into your hands
The husbandry and manage of my house
Until my lord's return: for mine own part,
I have toward heaven breathed a secret vow
To live in prayer and contemplation,
Only attended by Nerissa here,
Until her husband and my lord's return:
There is a monastery two miles off;
And there will we abide. I do desire you
Not to deny this imposition;
The which my love and some necessity
Now lays upon you.

LORENZO.

Madam, with all my heart;
I shall obey you in all fair commands.

PORTIA.

My people do already know my mind,
And will acknowledge you and Jessica
In place of Lord Bassanio and myself.
So fare you well, till we shall meet again.

LORENZO.

Fair thoughts and happy hours attend on you!

JESSICA.

I wish your ladyship all heart's content.

PORTIA.

I thank you for your wish, and am well pleased
To wish it back on you: fare you well, Jessica.

[*Exeunt* JESSICA *and* LORENZO.

Now, Balthazar,
As I have ever found thee honest-true,
So let me find thee still. Take this same letter,

21 **From out**：out of.
24 **commit**：entrust.
25 **husbandry**：house-keeping. **manage**：management.
30 **husband**：husband's，其's 和 lord's 共用。
31 **monastery**：修道院。
33 **deny**：refuse. **imposition**：injunction，charge，嘱托。
34 **The which**：which. **my love**；my friendship.
35 **lays**：imposes. **with…heart**：I am quite willing.
41 **attend on**：be with.
44 **on**：to.
46 **honest-true**：honest and true.
47 **same**：用于 this 后加强语气。

And use thou all the endeavour of a man
In speed to Padua: see thou render this
Into my cousin's hand, Doctor Bellario;
And, look, what notes and garments he doth give thee,
Bring them, I pray thee, with imagined speed
Unto the tranect, to the common ferry
Which trades to Venice. Waste no time in words,
But get thee gone: I shall be there before thee.

BALTHAZAR.

Madam, I go with all convenient speed. [*Exit*.

PORTIA.

Come on, Nerissa; I have work in hand
That you yet know not of: we'll see our husbands
Before they think of us.

NERISSA.

Shall they see us?

PORTIA.

They shall, Nerissa; but in such a habit,
That they shall think we are accomplished
With that we lack. I'll hold thee any wager,
When we are both accoutred like young men,
I'll prove the prettier fellow of the two,
And wear my dagger with the braver grace;
And speak between the change of man and boy
With a reed voice; and turn two mincing steps
Into a manly stride; and speak of frays,
Like a fine-bragging youth; and tell quaint lies,
How honourable ladies sought my love,
Which I denying, they fell sick and died,—
I could not do withal;— then I'll repent,
And wish, for all that, that I had not kill'd them:
And twenty of these puny lies I'll tell;
That men shall swear I have discontinued school
Above a twelvemonth:—I have within my mind

49 **see**：take care that. **render**：deliver.

50 Into the hand of my cousin，Doctor Bellario.

51 **look**：注意。 **what**：whatever. **notes**：papers and letters.

52 **imagined**：all imaginable.

53 **tranect**：ferry between the island of Venice and the mainland（意大利 traghetto）.

60 **habit**：costume.

61—62 **accomplished**：furnished，equipped. **that**：what. **we are…lack**：i.e. we are men.

63 **accoutred**[ˈəkuːtəd]：fully dressed.

65 **braver**：more gallant.

67 **reed voice**：shrill voice like the sound made by a reed. **mincing steps**：small steps，taken in an affected way，婀娜细步。

68 **frays**：brawls，fights，打架。

69 **quaint**：ingenious.

71 **Which I denying**：and when I refuse to give them my love.

72 **I could not do withal**：I could not deal with all of them.

73 **for**：in spite of.

74 **puny**：petty.

75 **That**：so that. **discontinued school**：left school，毕业，走出学校。

76 **Above a twelvemonth**：over a year.

A thousand raw tricks of these bragging Jacks,
Which I will practise.

NERISSA.

Why, shall we turn to men?

PORTIA.

Fie, what a question's that,
If thou wert near a lewd interpreter!
But come, I'll tell thee all my whole device
When I am in my coach, which stays for us
At the park-gate; and therefore haste away,
For we must measure twenty miles to-day. [*Exeunt*.

SCENE V

The same. A garden.

Enter LAUNCELOT *and* JESSICA.

LAUNCELOT.

Yes, truly; for, look you, the sins of the father are to be laid upon the children: therefore, I promise ye, I fear you. I was always plain with you, and so now I speak my agitation of the matter: therefore be o'good cheer; for, truly, I think you are damn'd. There is but one hope in it that can do you any good; and that is but a kind of bastard hope neither.

JESSICA.

And what hope is that, I pray thee?

LAUNCELOT.

Marry, you may partly hope that your father got you not, — that you are not the Jew's daughter.

JESSICA.

That were a kind of bastard hope, indeed: so the sins of my mother should be visited upon me.

LAUNCELOT.

77 **raw**: unskilled. **Jacks**: knaves. **bragging Jacks**: boasting fellows.

78 **turn to**: change into.

81 **device**: plan.

83 **haste**: hasten, hurry.

84 **measure**: travel.

III.v

1 **look you**: mind you.

2 **promise**: tell beforehand.

3 **fear**: fear for…,为…担心。 **plain**: plain-spoken,说直话。

4 **agitation**: 为 cogitation (thinking)之误。

5 **o'**: of. **be…cheer**: be cheerful. **damn'd**: 注意要下地狱。

7 **bastard**: adulterate, spurious,掺假的;假的。 **neither**: either 因受 but 的影响,为否定词。

9 **got**: begot,生。

11 **bastard**: 私生子的(与前面的 bastard 构成双关语)。

12 **visited**: punished.

Truly, then, I fear you are damn'd both by father and mother: thus when I shun Scylla, your father, I fall into Charybdis, your mother: well, you are gone both ways.

JESSICA.

I shall be saved by my husband; he hath made me a Christian.

LAUNCELOT.

Truly, the more to blame he: we were Christians enow before; e'en as many as could well live, one by another. This making of Christians will raise the price of hogs: if we grow all to be pork-eaters, we shall not shortly have a rasher on the coals for money.

JESSICA.

I'll tell my husband, Launcelot, what you say: here he comes.

Enter LORENZO.

LORENZO.

I shall grow jealous of you shortly, Launcelot, if you thus get my wife into corners.

JESSICA.

Nay, you need not fear us, Lorenzo: Launcelot and I are out. He tells me flatly, there's no mercy for me in heaven, because I am a Jew's daughter: and he says, you are no good member of the commonwealth; for, in converting Jews to Christians, you raise the price of pork.

LORENZO.

I shall answer that better to the commonwealth than you can the getting up of the negro's belly: the Moor's with child by you, Launcelot.

LAUNCELOT.

It is much that the Moor should be more than reason: but if she be less than an honest woman,

14—15 **Scylla**['silə]和**Charybdis**[kə'ribdis]：传说前者为意大利半岛南端的岩石，上栖女妖；后者则为墨西拿海峡对面靠近西西里岛的一个旋涡，两者夹峙对经过的船只构成威胁，使之左右为难。

16 **gone**：lost，ruined.

19 **the…he**：he is the more to blame.

20—21 **enow**：enough. **one by another**：一个挨着一个（形容人数多，很拥挤）。

22—23 **hogs**：pigs，pork. **grow all to be**：all become. **we…shortly**：very soon we shall not. **rasher**['ræʃə]：咸肉（或火腿）薄片。**on the coals**：烧在炉灶上。 **for money**：用钱（买到）。

27 **get…into corners**：和人进行密谈。

29 **are out**：have quarreled，have fallen out.

31 **member**：citizen. **commonwealth**：state，国家。

32 **converting**：使改变宗教信仰。

34 **answer…to**：对…负责。

35 **can**：answer to. **getting up**：swelling.

36 **Moor**：黑人。 **with child**：pregnant.

37—38 **more than reason**：more than is reasonable（超过常情）；chaste.

she is indeed more than I took her for.

LORENZO.

How every fool can play upon the world! I think the best grace of wit will shortly turn into silence, and discourse grow commendable in none only but parrots. —Go in, sirrah; bid them prepare for dinner.

LAUNCELOT.

That's done, sir; they have all stomachs.

LORENZO.

Goodly Lord, what a wit-snapper are you! then bid them prepare dinner.

LAUNCELOT.

That is done too, sir; only 'cover' is the word.

LORENZO.

Will you cover, then, sir?

LAUNCELOT.

Not so, sir, neither; I know my duty.

LORENZO.

Yet more quarrelling with occasion! Wilt thou show the whole wealth of thy wit in an instant? I pray thee, understand a plain man in his plain meaning: go to thy fellows, bid them cover the table, serve in the meat, and we will come in to dinner.

LAUNCELOT.

For the table, sir, it shall be served in; for the meat, sir, it shall be cover'd; for your coming in to dinner, sir, why, let it be as humours and conceits shall govern. [*Exit*.

LORENZO.

O dear discretion, how his words are suited!
The fool hath planted in his memory
An army of good words; and I do know
A many fools, that stand in better place,
Garnisht like him, that for a tricksy word

39 **more**：bigger 指怀孕。

40 **play upon the word**：做文字游戏。

41 **grace**：excellence.

42 **commendable**：praiseworthy. **only but**：except.

43 **sirrah**：称呼下属时的用语。

44 **stomachs**：appetites（Launcelot 故意误解 prepare for dinner “准备开饭”为“准备吃饭”）。

45 **Goodly**：good，gracious. **Lord**：God. **wit-snapper**：one who says spiteful things wittily.

47 **cover**：cover the table，spread the cloth for a meal.

49 **neither**：either. **I…duty**：I know my place as a servant，I shall not cover my head（wear my hat）before my superiors.

50 **quarrelling**：quibbling，说双关语。 **with occasion**：on every occasion.

55 **For**：as regards.

57 **humours**：inclinations. **conceits**：thoughts.

60 **discretion**：good sense，wisdom. **suited**：matched，forced to suit his purpose.

61—65 据认为此段系莎士比亚对演丑角（包括 Launcelot）的同行 William Kempe 的赞誉。

63 **A many**：many 是古英语名词，后面省略 of.

64 **Garnisht**：furnished，supplied（with words）. **tricksy**：smart，俏皮的。

Defy the matter.—How cheer'st thou, Jessica?
And now, good sweet, say thy opinion,—
How dost thou like the Lord Bassanio's wife?

JESSICA.

Past all expressing. It is very meet
The Lord Bassanio live an upright life;
For, having such a blessing in his lady,
He finds the joys of heaven here on earth;
And if on earth he do not mean it, then
In reason he should never come to heaven.
Why, if two gods should play some heavenly match,
And on the wager lay two earthly women,
And Portia one, there must be something else
Pawn'd with the other; for the poor rude world
Hath not her fellow.

LORENZO.

Even such a husband
Hast thou of me as she is for a wife.

JESSICA.

Nay, but ask my opinion too of that.

LORENZO.

I will anon: first, let us go to dinner.

JESSICA.

Nay, let me praise you while I have a stomach.

LORENZO.

No, prithee, let it serve for table-talk;
Then, howsoe'er thou speak'st, 'mong other things
I shall digest it.

JESSICA.

Well, I'll set you forth. [*Exeunt*.

65 **Defy the matter**: refuse to elucidate the subject under discussion. **cheer'st**: fare.

66 **sweet**: sweetheart.

68 **Past all expressing**: beyond words. **meet**(adj.): proper, fitting.

72 **mean**: 很多评注家认为此字系 merit 之误。

75 **lay**: depend.

76 **something**: someone.

77 **Pawn'd**: staked.

78 **fellow**: equal, match.

79 **of**: in.

82 **stomach**: appetite, desire for it.

84 **'mong**: together with.

85 **set you forth**: praise you greatly.

ACT IV

SCENE I

Venice. A court of justice.

Enter the DUKE, *the* MAGNIFICOES, ANTONIO, BASSANIO, GRATIANO, SOLANIO, SALARINO, *and others.*

DUKE OF VENICE.

What, is Antonio here?

ANTONIO.

Ready, so please your Grace.

DUKE OF VENICE.

I am sorry for thee: thou art come to answer
A stony adversary, an inhuman wretch
Uncapable of pity, void and empty
From any dram of mercy.

ANTONIO.

I have heard
Your Grace hath ta'en great pains to qualify
His rigorous course; but since he stands obdurate,
And that no lawful means can carry me
Out of his envy's reach, I do oppose
My patience to his fury; and am arm'd
To suffer, with a quietness of spirit,
The very tyranny and rage of his.

DUKE OF VENICE.

Go one, and call the Jew into the court.

SOLANIO.

He's ready at the door: he comes, my lord.

Enter SHYLOCK.

DUKE OF VENICE.

IV.i

2 **Ready**：(the standard answer in court) 有。 **your Grace**：殿下。

5 **Uncapable**：incapable.

6 **From**：of. **dram**：drop，minute quantity.

7 **pains**：efforts. **qualify**：moderate，soften.

8 **course**：course of legal action，proceedings.

9 **that**：和 since 同位。

10 **envy**：malice.

11 **arm'd**：equipped，prepared.

13 **tyranny**：violence.

14 **Go one**：Let one go.

Make room, and let him stand before our face.—
Shylock, the world thinks, and I think so too,
That thou but lead'st this fashion of thy malice
To the last hour of act; and then 'tis thought
Thou'lt show thy mercy and remorse more strange
Than is thy strange apparent cruelty;
And where thou now exact'st the penalty,—
Which is a pound of this poor merchant's flesh,—
Thou wilt not only loose the forfeiture,
But, toucht with human gentleness and love,
Forgive a moiety of the principal;
Glancing an eye of pity on his losses,
That have of late so huddled on his back,
Enow to press a royal merchant down,
And pluck commiseration of his state
From brassy bosoms and rough hearts of flint,
From stubborn Turks and Tartars, never train'd
To offices of tender courtesy.
We all expect a gentle answer, Jew.

SHYLOCK.

I have possest your Grace of what I purpose;
And by our holy Sabbath have I sworn
To have the due and forfeit of my bond:
If you deny it, let the danger light
Upon your charter and your city's freedom.
You'll ask me, why I rather choose to have
A weight of carrion-flesh than to receive
Three thousand ducats: I'll not answer that;
But say it is my humour: is it answer'd?
What if my house be troubled with a rat,
And I be pleased to give ten thousand ducats
To have it baned! What, are you answer'd yet?
Some men there are love not a gaping pig;
Some, that are mad if they behold a cat;

18 **but**：only. **lead'st**：carry. **fashion**：mere form，pretence.

19 **act**：action.

20 **remorse**：pity，compassion. **strange**：unusual.

21 **strange**：unnatural. **apparent**：clear，manifest.

22 **where**：whereas.

24 **loose**：release，give up. **forfeiture**：penalty.

26 **Forgive**：let go. **moiety**：part，portion.

27 **his losses**：the losses of him.

28 **That**：who. **huddled**：crowded，been heaped (piled).

29 **Enow**[i'nau]：enough. **royal merchant**：见 III. ii 239 行。

32 **Turks and Tartars**：土耳其人和鞑靼人（They were looked upon by the Europeans as savage and cruel people).

33 **offices**：services，actions. **courtesy**：kindness.

35 **possest**：informed. **purpose**(v.i.)：intend to do.

36 **by our holy Sabbath**['sæbəθ]：发誓语（Sabbath 为犹太人的安息日"主日"，在星期六）。

37 **due and forfeit**：debt and penalty.

38 **light**(v.i.)：fall.

39 **charter**：document embodying the constitution of a city，城邦国家的宪法。 **freedom**：civic rights.

41 **carrion-flesh**：臭肉。

43 **humour**：inclination.

46 **baned**：poisoned.

47 **love**：前省略 who. **gaping pig**：suckling pig served with a fruit in its wide-open mouth.

48 **are mad**：become wildly agitated.

And others, when the bag-pipe sings i' th' nose,
Cannot contain their urine: for affection,
Mistress of passion, sways it to the mood
Of what it likes or loathes. Now, for your answer:
As there is no firm reason to be render'd,
Why he cannot abide a gaping pig;
Why he, a harmless necessary cat;
Why he, a woollen bag-pipe,—but of force
Must yield to such inevitable shame
As to offend himself, being offended;
So can I give no reason, nor I will not,
More than a lodged hate and a certain loathing
I bear Antonio, that I follow thus
A losing suit against him. Are you answer'd?

BASSANIO.

This is no answer, thou unfeeling man,
To excuse the current of thy cruelty.

SHYLOCK.

I am not bound to please thee with my answer.

BASSANIO.

Do all men kill the things they do not love?

SHYLOCK.

Hates any man the thing he would not kill?

BASSANIO.

Every offence is not a hate at first.

SHYLOCK.

What, would'st thou have a serpent sting thee twice?

ANTONIO.

I pray you, think you question with the Jew:
You may as well go stand upon the beach,
And bid the main flood bate his usual height;
You may as well use question with the wolf,
Why he hath made the ewe bleat for the lamb;

49 bag-pipe：苏格兰风笛。 **sings i' th' nose**：sings in the nose，响出鼻音一样的音乐。

50 affection：natural inclination，one's likes and dislikes.

51 Mistress：为 affection 的同位语。 **sways**：moves，directs. **it**：代 passion.

52 it：代 affection.

53 render'd：given.

54—56 he…he…he：this one…that one…another. **abide**：bear，put up with. **necessary**：for keeping down mice.

56 woollen：covered with woollen cloth. **of force**：by necessity.

57 Must：此前的主语 he 省略。

59 nor…not：nor will I.

60 lodged：deep-seated. **certain**：sure，fixed.

61 that：so that.

62 losing suit：unprofitable suit，in which I stand to lose a lot of money.

64 current：course.

68 Every…first：（部分否定）Not every offence is a hate at first.

70 think：consider，take into consideration. **question**：argue.

72 main flood：ocean. **bate**：abate，lower. **his**：its.

73 use question：argue.

You may as well forbid the mountain pines
To wag their high tops, and to make no noise,
When they are fretten with the gusts of heaven;
You may as well do any thing most hard,
As seek to soften that,—than which what's hareder? —
His Jewish heart:—therefore, I do beseech you,
Make no more offers, use no further means,
But, with all brief and plain conveniency,
Let me have judgement, and the Jew his will.

BASSANIO.

For thy three thousand ducats here is six.

SHYLOCK.

If every ducat in six thousand ducats
Were in six parts, and every part a ducat,
I would not draw them,—I would have my bond.

DUKE OF VENICE.

How shalt thou hope for mercy, rendering none?

SHYLOCK.

What judgement shall I dread, doing no wrong?
You have among you many a purchased slave,
Which, like your asses and your dogs and mules,
You use in abject and in slavish parts
Because you bought them:—shall I say to you,
Let them be free, marry them to your heirs?
Why sweat they under burdens? let their beds
Be made as soft as yours, and let their palates
Be season'd with such viands? You will answer,
The slaves are ours:—so do I answer you:
The pound of flesh, which I demand of him,
Is dearly bought, 'tis mine, and I will have it.
If you deny me, fie upon your law!
There is no force in the decrees of Venice.
I stand for judgement: answer,—shall I have it?

76 **to make**：前省略 bid them；另一种意见认为是 forbid them to make no noise，两个否定仍为否定。

77 **fretten with**：fretted by，tossed by.

78 **hard**：difficult.

82 **all**：most. **with … conveniency**：with the greatest speed and convenience.

87 **draw**：take.

91 **Which**：who.

92 **use**：employ. **parts**：services，tasks.

97 **season'd**：given a pleasing savour. **with such viands**['vaiədz]：by foods such as yours.

101 **fie**：（感叹词）disgust.

DUKE OF VENICE.
Upon my power I may dismiss this court,
Unless Bellario, a learned doctor,
Whom I have sent for to determine this,
Come here to-day.

SOLANIO.
My lord, here stays without
A messenger with letters from the doctor,
New come from Padua.

DUKE OF VENICE.
Bring us the letters; call the messenger.

BASSANIO.
Good cheer, Antonio! What, man, courage yet!
The Jew shall have my flesh, blood, bones, and all,
Ere thou shalt lose for me one drop of blood.

ANTONIO.
I am a tainted wether of the flock,
Meetest for death: the weakest kind of fruit
Drops earliest to the ground; and so let me:
You cannot better be employ'd, Bassanio,
Than to live still, and write mine epitaph.

Enter NERISSA, *dressed like a lawyer's clerk.*

DUKE OF VENICE.
Came you from Padua, from Bellario?

NERISSA.
From both, my lord. Bellario greets your Grace.
[*Presents a letter.*

BASSANIO.
Why dost thou whet thy knife so earnestly?

SHYLOCK.
To cut the forfeiture from that bankrout there.

GRATIANO.
Not on thy sole, but on thy soul, harsh Jew,
Thou makest thy knife keen; but no metal can,

104 **upon**：in accordance with.

107 **stays**：waits. **without**：outside.

109 **New**：newly，recently. **come**(p.p.)：修饰 messenger.

111 **Good cheer**：courage! Be of good heart! **What**：well.(感叹词) **courage**：have courage.

114 **tainted**：diseased. **wether**：gelded sheep.

115 **Meetest**：most fit.

122 **bankrout**：bankrupt，破产者。

123 **sole**，**soul**：同音词的文字游戏。

No, not the hangman's axe, bear half the keenness
Of thy sharp envy. Can no prayers pierce thee?

SHYLOCK.

No, none that thou hast wit enough to make.

GRATIANO.

O, be thou damn'd, inexecrable dog!
And for thy life let justice be accused.
Thou almost makest me waver in my faith,
To hold opinion with Pythagoras,
That souls of animals infuse themselves
Into the trunks of men: thy currish spirit
Govern'd a wolf, who, hang'd for human slaughter,
Even from the gallows did his fell soul fleet,
And, whilst thou lay'st in thy unhallow'd dam,
Infused itself in thee; for thy desires
Are wolvish, bloody, starved, and ravenous.

SHYLOCK.

Till thou canst rail the seal from off my bond,
Thou but offend'st thy lungs to speak so loud:
Repair thy wit, good youth, or it will fall
To cureless ruin.—I stand here for law.

DUKE OF VENICE.

This letter from Bellario doth commend
A young and learned doctor to our court.—
Where is he?

NERISSA.

He attendeth here hard by,
To know your answer, whether you'll admit him.

DUKE OF VENICE.

With all my heart.—Some three or four of you
Go give him courteous conduct to this place.—
Meantime the court shall hear Bellario's letter.

CLERK [*reads*].

Your Grace shall understand, that at the receipt of

126 **envy**：ill-will，malice.

128 **inexecrable**[inˈeksikrəbl]：most execrable (detestable)，试比较 invaluable 等于 most valuable.

129 **for…accused**：justice must be blamed if it allows you to live on.

130 **faith**：religion.

131 **hold opinion with**：agree to the opinion of. **Pythagoras**[paiˈθæɡəræs]：首倡轮回说的古希腊哲学家。

132 **infuse themselves into**：渗入。

134 **wolf**：此处莎士比亚可能影射被指控阴谋毒害伊丽莎白女王而于 1594 年 6 月 7 日处死的犹太医生罗德里戈·洛佩斯(Lopez，拉丁字源 lupus 意为"狼")。

135 **fell**：cruel，deadly. **fleet**：fly，pass rapidly.

136 **unhallowed**：unholy，impious. **dam**：鸟兽之母(用于指人时表示轻蔑，指犹如母兽一般)。

139 **rail**：谩骂。

140 **offend'st**：injure.

141 **Repair**：restore to good condition. **or**：otherwise.

142 **cureless ruin**：insanity，madness.

143 **commend**：recommend，推荐。

145 **attendeth**：is waiting. **hard by**：near by.

148 **give…conduct**：conduct him (bring him in) courteously.

150 **shall**：is to. **at…of**：on receiving.

your letter I am very sick: but in the instant that your messenger came, in loving visitation was with me a young doctor of Rome; his name is Balthazar. I acquainted him with the cause in controversy between the Jew and Antonio the merchant: we turn'd o'er many books together: he is furnisht with my opinion; which, better'd with his own learning, — the greatness whereof I cannot enough commend, — comes with him, at my importunity, to fill up your Grace's request in my stead. I beseech you, let his lack of years be no impediment to let him lack a reverend estimation; for I never knew so young a body with so old a head. I leave him to your gracious acceptance, whose trial shall better publish his commendation.

DUKE OF VENICE.

You hear the learn'd Bellario, what he writes:
And here, I take it, is the doctor come.

Enter PORTIA *for* BALTHAZAR.

Give me your hand. Come you from old Bellario?

PORTIA.

I did, my lord.

DUKE OF VENICE.

You are welcom: take your place.
Are you acquainted with the difference
That holds this present question in the court?

PORTIA.

I am informed throughly of the cause.—
Which is the merchant here, and which the Jew?

DUKE OF VENICE.

Antonio and old Shylock, both stand forth.

PORTIA.

Is your name Shylock?

SHYLOCK.

151 **in the instant that**: at the time when.

152 **in loving visitation**: on a friendly visit.

157 **better'd**: improved.

158 **whereof**: of which (his learning).

159 **importunity**: urgent request. **fill up**: comply with.

160—161 **in my stead**: instead of me, in my place. **to let his lack**: to cause him to lack.

164 **whose trial**: the test of him. **publish**: proclaim.

166 **the…writes**: what the learned Bellario writes.

171 **difference**: divergence of opinion.

172 **holds**: keeps. **question**: lawsuit.

173 **throughly**: thoroughly.

Shylock is my name.

PORTIA.

Of a strange nature is the suit you follow;
Yet in such rule, that the Venetian law
Cannot impugn you as you do proceed.—
You stand within his danger, do you not?

ANTONIO.

Ay, so he says.

PORTIA.

Do you confess the bond?

ANTONIO.

I do.

PORTIA.

Then must the Jew be merciful.

SHYLOCK.

On what compulsion must I? tell me that.

PORTIA.

The quality of mercy is not strain'd,—
It droppeth as the gentle rain from heaven
Upon the place beneath: it is twice blest,—
It blesseth him that gives, and him that takes:
'Tis mightiest in the mightiest: it becomes
The throned monarch better than his crown;
His sceptre shows the force of temporal power,
The attribute to awe and majesty,
Wherein doth sit the dread and fear of kings;
But mercy is above this sceptred sway,—
It is enthroned in the hearts of kings,
It is an attribute to God himself;
And earthly power doth then show likest God's
When mercy seasons justice. Therefore, Jew,
Though justice be thy plea, consider this,—
That, in the course of justice, none of us
Should see salvation: we do pray for mercy;

177 **suit**: lawauit. **follow**: pursue,从事。

178 **in such rule**: so far in order.

179 **impugn**: oppose, counteract,驳回。

180 此句转向 Antonio 说。 **within his danger**: in his power, in his debt.

182 **must the Jew be**: the Jew is to be.

183 **compulsion**: compelling account.

184 **strain'd**: under compulsion, forced.这里开始,是著名的关于"mercy"的演说。mercy 一词可有两种不同的释义:①misericordia,慈悲,善心;②clemency,宽大。根据不同的上下文,请读者自己体会其含义。

188 **becomes**: befits, suits.

190 **temporal**: pertaining to this life or this world.

191 **attribute to**: essential quality ascribed to,主要体现着…的性质。 **awe**: reverential fear,敬畏。 **majesty**: royalty,王权。

193 **sceptred sway**: power of the king.

196 **likest**: most like.

197 **seasons**: tempers, flavours.

199 **That**: 引导和 this 同位的从句。

200 **salvation**: 灵魂得救。按基督教的原罪说,人本要沉沦下地狱,只是靠了神恩(God's grace, mercy)才能得救,灵魂上天堂。

And that same prayer doth teach us all to render
The deeds of mercy. I have spoke thus much
To mitigate the justice of thy plea;
Which if thou follow, this strict court of Venice
Must needs give sentence 'gainst the merchant there.

SHYLOCK.

My deeds upon my head! I crave the law,
The penalty and forfeit of my bond.

PORTIA.

Is he not able to discharge the money?

BASSANIO.

Yes, here I tender it for him in the court;
Yea, thrice the sum: if that will not suffice,
I will be bound to pay it ten times o'er,
On forfeit of my hands, my head, my heart:
If this will not suffice, it must appear
That malice bears down truth. And I beseech you,
Wrest once the law to your authority:
To do a great right, do a little wrong;
And curb this cruel devil of his will.

PORTIA.

It must not be; there is no power in Venice
Can alter a decree established:
'Twill be recorded for a precedent;
And many an error, by the same example,
Will rush into the state: it cannot be.

SHYLOCK.

A Daniel come to judgement! yea, a Daniel! —
O wise young judge, how I do honour thee!

PORTIA.

I pray you, let me look upon the bond.

SHYLOCK.

Here 'tis, most reverend doctor, here it is.

PORTIA.

201 that same prayer: the Lord's Prayer,主祷文,见《圣经·新约·马太福音》第6章9—13节。其中有这样的话:"免我们的债,如同我们免了人的债"。 **render**: pay back.

202 spoke: spoken.

203 mitigate…plea: temper (soften) your insistence on strict justice.

204 follow: pursue.

206 My…head!: Let the consequence of my doings fall on my head; I'll answer for my deeds,我做的事,后果自负。 **crave**: desire; demand.

208 discharge: pay off,偿付。

209 tender: offer.

212 On forfeit of: on penalty of,如违认罚舍割。

214 bears down: overpowers, conquers,征服。

215 Wrest: twist, bend. **Wrest…authority**: 利用你的权力把法律稍许变通一下。

217 curb…will: restrain this cruel Jew from his will.

219 Can: 前面省略 that.

220 for: as.

223 Daniel: 古犹太有名的年轻法官,见《圣经》苏珊娜与长老的故事等。 **come**(p.p.):前面省略 is 或 has.

224 thee: 这里因感叹修辞而用,和251行同。Shylock 直接对 Portia 说话时用 you,如236—239行。

Shylock, there's thrice thy money offer'd thee.

SHYLOCK.

An oath, an oath, I have an oath in heaven:
Shall I lay perjury upon my soul?
No, not for Venice.

PORTIA.

Why, this bond is forfeit;
And lawfully by this the Jew may claim
A pound of flesh, to be by him cut off
Nearest the merchant's heart.—Be merciful:
Take thrice thy money; bid me tear the bond.

SHYLOCK.

When it is paid according to the tenour.—
It doth appear you are a worthy judge;
You know the law, your exposition
Hath been most sound: I charge you by the law,
Whereof you are a well-deserving pillar,
Proceed to judgement: by my soul I swear
There is no power in the tongue of man
To alter me: I stay here on my bond.

ANTONIO.

Most heartily I do beseech the court
To give the judgement.

PORTIA.

Why then, thus it is:—
You must prepare your bosom for his knife.

SHYLOCK.

O noble judge! O excellent young man!

PORTIA.

For the intent and purpose of the law
Hath full relation to the penalty,
Which here appeareth due upon the bond.

SHYLOCK.

'Tis very true: O wise and upright judge!

230 **for Venice**: in exchange for Venice,把威尼斯作为交换条件。**forfeit**(adj.): breached, transgressed.

235 **tenour**: purport, sense contained (in the bond), terms.

237 **exposition**: interpretation.

241 **tongue**: language.

242 **To alter me**: that can alter my decision. **on**: in dependence on.

248 **Hath…to**: is in full accord with.

How much more elder art thou than thy looks!

PORTIA.

Therefore lay bare your bosom.

SHYLOCK.

Ay, his breast:
So says the bond:—doth it not, noble judge? —
Nearest his heart: those are the very words.

PORTIA.

It is so. Are there balance here to weigh
The flesh?

SHYLOCK.

I have them ready.

PORTIA.

Have by some surgeon, Shylock, on your charge,
To stop his wounds, lest he do bleed to death.

SHYLOCK.

Is it so nominated in the bond?

PORTIA.

It is not so exprest: but what of that?
'Twere good you do so much for charity.

SHYLOCK.

I cannot find it; 'tis not in the bond.

PORTIA.

You, merchant, have you any thing to say?

ANTONIO.

But little: I am arm'd and well prepared.—
Give me your hand, Bassanio: fare you well!
Grieve not that I am fall'n to this for you;
For herein Fortune shows herself more kind
Than is her custom: it is still her use
To let the wretched man outlive his wealth,
To view with hollow eye and wrinkled brow
An age of poverty; from which lingering penance
Of such a misery doth she cut me off.

251 more elder：older 当时常用双重比较级。

255 balance：scales 用作复数。

257 by：on hand，nearby. **on your charge**：at your expense.

259 nominated：mentioned，laid down.

260 what of that?：What does it matter?

261 'Twere：It would be.

266 am fall'n to this：have got into such a condition.

267 Fortune：命运女神。

268 still：always. **use**：usual way.

271 age：old age. **which**：this.

Commend me to your honourable wife:
Tell her the process of Antonio's end;
Say how I loved you, speak me fair in death;
And, when the tale is told, bid her be judge
Whether Bassanio had not once a love.
Repent but you that you shall lose your friend,
And he repents not that he pays your debt;
For, if the Jew do cut but deep enough,
I'll pay it presently with all my heart.

BASSANIO.

Antonio, I am married to a wife
Which is as dear to me as life itself;
But life itself, my wife, and all the world,
Are not with me esteem'd above thy life:
I would lose all, ay, sacrifice them all
Here to this devil, to deliver you.

PORTIA.

Your wife would give you little thanks for that,
If she were by, to hear you make the offer.

GRATIANO.

I have a wife, whom, I protest, I love:
I would she were in heaven, so she could
Entreat some power to change this currish Jew.

NERISSA.

'Tis well you offer it behind her back;
The wish would make else an unquiet house.

SHYLOCK [*aside*].

These be the Christian husbands! I have a daughter;
Would any of the stock of Barabbas
Had been her husband rather than a Christian! —
We trifle time: I pray thee, pursue sentence.

PORTIA.

A pound of that same merchant's flesh is thine:
The court awards it, and the law doth give it.

274 **process**：双关语 1.manner；2.legal process。 **end**：death.

275 **speak me fair**：speak well (favourably) of me.

277 **love**：dear friend.

278 **Repent but you**：feel sorry only.

281 **with all my heart**：双关语 1.用我的整个心脏；2.十分乐意地。

283 **Which**：who.

285 **with**：by.

287 **to deliver**：in order to deliver.

289 **by**：near by，present.

290 **protest**：assert publicly，declare.

294 **else**：otherwise. **make…house**：make your wife quarrel with you all the time.

296 **Would**：I wish. **stock**：family，breed. **Barabbas**：作乱杀人犯，和耶稣同为囚犯。祭司长唆众将其释放，而耶稣则被钉十字架而死。见《圣经·新约·马可福音》第 15 章 7—15 节。

298 **trifle time**：waste time in trifles. **pursue sentence**：作出判决。

300 **awards**：decrees，判给。

SHYLOCK.

Most rightful judge!

PORTIA.

And you must cut this flesh from off his breast:
The law allows it, and the court awards it.

SHYLOCK.

Most learned judge! —A sentence! come, prepare!

PORTIA.

Tarry a little; there is something else.
This bond doth give thee here no jot of blood,—
The words expressly are,'a pound of flesh':
Take then thy bond, take thou thy pound of flesh;
But, in the cutting it, if thou dost shed
One drop of Christian blood,thy lands and goods
Are, by the laws of Venice, confiscate
Unto the state of Venice.

GRATIANO.

O upright judge! —Mark, Jew:—O learned judge!

SHYLOCK.

Is that the law?

PORTIA.

Thyself shalt see the act:
For, as thou urgest justice, be assured
Thou shalt have justice, more than thou desirest.

GRATIANO.

O learned judge! —Mark,Jew:—a learned judge!

SHYLOCK.

I take his offer, then;—pay the bond thrice,
And let the Christian go.

BASSANIO.

Here is the money.

PORTIA.

Soft!
The Jew shall have all justice;—soft! no haste:—

301 rightful：just.

305 Tarry：wait.

306 jot：small drop.

308 take…thy bond：take the right given by the bond.参看 III. iii 4 行。

309 the cutting it：这是英语中从 the cutting of it 到 cutting it 简化过程中的一个中间形式。

311 confiscate：confiscated,被没收。在 t 音后,ed 常省略。

312 state：Venice was then a city state.

313 Mark：注意。

314 act：legal document.

320 Soft!：stay，stop.

He shall have nothing but the penalty.

GRATIANO.

O Jew! an upright judge, a learned judge!

PORTIA.

Therefore prepare thee to cut off the flesh.
Shed thou no blood; nor cut thou less nor more
But just a pound of flesh: if thou cutt'st more
Or less than a just pound,—be it but so much
As makes it light or heavy in the substance,
Or the division of the twentieth part
Of one poor scruple, nay, if the scale do turn
But in the estimation of a hair,—
Thou diest, and all thy goods are confiscate.

GRATIANO.

A second Daniel, a Daniel, Jew!
Now, infidel, I have you on the hip.

PORTIA.

Why doth the Jew pause? take thy forfeiture.

SHYLOCK.

Give me my principal, and let me go.

BASSANIO.

I have it ready for thee; here it is.

PORTIA.

He hath refused it in the open court:
He shall have merely justice and his bond.

GRATIANO.

A Daniel, still say I, a second Daniel! —
I thank thee, Jew, for teaching me that word.

SHYLOCK.

Shall I not have barely my principal?

PORTIA.

Thou shalt have nothing but the forfeiture,
To be so taken at thy peril, Jew.

SHYLOCK.

326 just a pound：an exact pound.

328 substance：total weight.

330 scruple：a small unit of weight in ancient Rome.

331 estimation：estimated weight.

332 confiscate：confiscated.参看 311 行。

334 I…hip：I have you at my mercy.参看 I.iii 42 行。

342 barely：merely.

344 peril：risk.

Why, then the devil give him good of it!
I'll stay no longer question.

PORTIA.

Tarry, Jew:
The law hath yet another hold on you.
It is enacted in the laws of Venice,—
If it be proved against an alien
That by direct or indirect attempts
He seek the life of any citizen,
The party 'gainst the which he doth contrive
Shall seize one half his goods; the other half
Comes to the privy coffer of the state;
And the offender's life lies in the mercy
Of the duke only, 'gainst all other voice.
In which predicament, I say, thou stand'st;
For it appears, by manifest proceeding,
That indirectly, and directly too,
Thou hast contrived against the very life
Of the defendant; and thou hast incurr'd
The danger formerly by me rehearsed.
Down, therefore, and beg mercy of the duke.

GRATIANO.

Beg that thou mayst have leave to hang thyself:
And yet, thy wealth being forfeit to the state,
Thou hast not left the value of a cord;
Therefore thou must be hang'd at the state's charge.

DUKE OF VENICE.

That thou shalt see the difference of our spirits,
I pardon thee thy life before thou ask it:
For half thy wealth, it is Antonio's;
The other half comes to the general state,
Which humbleness may drive unto a fine.

PORTIA.

Ay, for the state,—not for Antonio.

345 **the…it!**：让魔鬼给他好处！

346 **I'll…question**：I'll remain here no longer to be questioned.

347 **hold**(n.)：grasp，把柄。

349 **alien**：foreigner.

351 **seek**：假设语气。 **citizen**：of the city state of Venice.

352 **the party**：那一方。（法律用语） **the which**：whom. **contrive**：plot evil，谋害。

354 **privy coffer**：secluded treasury.

355 **in**：at.

356 **'gainst**：in opposition to.

358 **manifest**：evident.

362 **rehearsed**：related.

363 **Down**：kneel down.

366 **left**(p.p.)：修饰 value. **cord**：rope for hanging.

367 **charge**：expense.

368 **That**：in order that（引导目的状语从句）。 **shalt**：will, may.

370 **For**：as regards.

371 **general**：public.

372 **humbleness**：humility and repentance. **drive**：reduce. **fine**：罚款。

SHYLOCK.

Nay, take my life and all; pardon not that:
You take my house, when you do take the prop
That doth sustain my house; you take my life,
When you to take the means whereby I live.

PORTIA.

What mercy can you render him, Antonio?

GRATIANO.

A halter gratis; nothing else, for God's sake.

ANTONIO.

So please my lord the duke and all the court
To quit the fine for one half of his goods,
I am content; so he will let me have
The other half in use, to render it,
Upon his death, unto the gentleman
That lately stole his daughter:
Two things provided more,—that, for this favour,
He presently become a Christian;
The other, that he do record a gift,
Here in the court, of all he dies possest,
Unto his son Lorenzo and his daughter.

DUKE OF VENICE.

He shall do this; or else I do recant
The pardon that I late pronounced here.

PORTIA.

Art thou contented, Jew? what dost thou say?

SHYLOCK.

I am content.

PORTIA.

Clerk, draw a deed of gift.

SHYLOCK.

I pray you, give me leave to go from hence;
I am not well: send the deed after me,
And I will sign it.

375 **prop**：栋梁（这里指钱财）。

377 **means**：wealth.

379 **halter gratis**：free rope for hanging.

381 **quit**：remit，免除。

382 **so**：provided that.

383 **in use**：in present possession，in trust，由……掌管。

386 **Two … more**：on condition of two more things，还有两个条件。 **for**：in exchange for.

387 **presently**：at once.

388 **record**：set down in writing.

389 **all … possest**：all the property he has at the time of his death. 从语法上讲，all 后省略 of which.

390 **son**：son-in-law.

391 **recant**：retract；take back.

392 **that**：what. **late**：just now.

394 **deed of gift**：赠送财产的文契。

DUKE OF VENICE.

Get thee gone, but do it.

GRATIANO.

In christening shalt thou have two godfathers:
Had I been judge, thou shouldst have had ten more,
To bring thee to the gallows, not the font.

[*Exit* SHYLOCK.

DUKE OF VENICE.

Sir, I entreat you home with me to dinner.

PORTIA.

I humbly do desire your Grace of pardon:
I must away this night toward Padua,
And it is meet I presently set forth.

DUKE OF VENICE.

I am sorry that your leisure serves you not.—
Antonio, gratify this gentleman;
For, in my mind, you are much bound to him.

[*Exeunt* DUKE *and his* TRAIN.

BASSANIO.

Most worthy gentleman, I and my friend
Have by your wisdom been this day acquitted
Of grievous penalties; in lieu whereof
Three thousand ducats, due unto the Jew,
We freely cope your courteous pains withal.

ANTONIO.

And stand indebted, over and above,
In love and service to you evermore.

PORTIA.

He is well paid that is well satisfied;
And I, delivering you, am satisfied,
And therein do account myself well paid:
My mind was never yet more mercenary.
I pray you, know me when we meet again:
I wish you well, and so I take my leave.

399 **thou…more**: i.e. to form a jury of twelve men.

400 **font**: 洗礼盘。

402 **desire your Grace of pardon**: desire pardon from your Grace.

403 **away**: go away.

404 **meet**: proper.

405 **your…not**: you have no spare time，不得空。

406 **gratify**: be courteous to (a polite way of saying "reward").

407 **bound**: in debt, obliged.

409—410 **acquitted/Of**: set free from.

410 **grievous**: painful. **in lieu whereof**: in return for it.

412 **cope**: give in compensation for, requite.

413 **over and above**: first of all.

415 **that**: who.

417 **account**: consider.

418 **mercenary**: interested in money.

419 **know…again**: a polite phrase meaning "I hope we shall see more of each other."

BASSANIO.

Dear sir, of force I must attempt you further:
Take some remembrance of us, as a tribute,
Not as a fee: grant me two things, I pray you,—
Not to deny me, and to pardon me.

PORTIA.

You press me far, and therefore I will yield.
[*to* ANTONIO]Give me your gloves, I'll wear them for your sake;
[*to* BASSANIO]And, for your love, I'll take this ring from you:—
Do not draw back your hand; I'll take no more;
And you in love shall not deny me this.

BASSANIO.

This ring, good sir,—alas, it is a trifle!
I will not shame myself to give you this.

PORTIA.

I will have nothing else but only this;
And now methinks I have a mind to it.

BASSANIO.

There's more depends on this than on the value,
The dearest ring in Venice will I give you,
And find it out by proclamation:
Only for this, I pray you, pardon me.

PORTIA.

I see, sir, you are liberal in offers:
You taught me first to beg; and now methinks
You teach me how a beggar should be answer'd.

BASSANIO.

Good sir, this ring was given me by my wife;
And, when she put it on, she made me vow
That I should neither sell nor give nor lose it.

PORTIA.

That 'scuse serves many men to save their gifts.

421 **of…further**：I am forced to try to make another request of you.

422 **remembrance**：memento，纪念品。 **of**：from. **tribute**：anything given out of devotion，表示敬意的礼物。

423 **fee**：reward.

427 **for your love**：as a keepsake for your friendship.

431 **shame myself**：make myself ashamed. **to give**：by giving.

433 **have…to**：like.

436 **proclamation**：notice given to the public，公告。

444 **'scuse**：excuse.

An if your wife be not a mad-woman,
And know how well I have deserved this ring,
She would not hold out enemy for ever
For giving it to me. Well, peace be with you!
[*Exeunt* PORTIA *and* NERISSA.

ANTONIO.
My Lord Bassanio, let him have the ring:
Let his deservings, and my love withal,
Be valued 'gainst your wife's commandment.

BASSANIO.
Go, Gratiano, run and overtake him;
Give him this ring; and bring him, if thou canst,
Unto Antonio's house:—away! make haste.
[*Exit* GRATIANO.
Come, you and I will thither presently;
And in the morning early will we both
Fly toward Belmont: come, Antonio. [*Exeunt*.

SCENE II

The same. A street.

Enter PORTIA *and* NERISSA.

PORTIA.
Inquire the Jew's house out, give him this deed,
And let him sign it: we'll away to-night,
And be a day before our husbands home:
This deed will be well welcome to Lorenzo.

Enter GRATIANO.

GRATIANO.
Fair sir, you are well o'erta'en:
My Lord Bassanio, upon more advice,
Hath sent you here this ring; and doth entreat
Your company at dinner.

445 An if: if.

447 hold out enemy: persist in quarreling with you.

448 peace…you!:(告别语)祝你们一路平安!

450 deservings: deserts,功劳。 **withal**: at the same time.

451 commandment: command.

IV.ii

3 home(adv.):到家。

5 Fair: good. **you…o'erta'en**: I am lucky to have overtaken you.

6 upon more advice: on further consideration.

7—8 entreat…dinner: beg you to come to dinner.

PORTIA.

That cannot be:
His ring I do accept most thankfully;
And so, I pray you, tell him: furthermore,
I pray you, show my youth old Shylock's house.

GRATIANO.

That will I do.

NERISSA.

Sir, I would speak with you.—
[*to* PORTIA]I'll see if I can get my husband's ring,
Which I did make him swear to keep for ever.

PORTIA [*to* NERISSA].

Thou mayst, I warrant. We shall have old swearing
That they did give the rings away to men;
But we'll outface them, and outswear them too.—
Away! make haste: thou know'st where I will tarry.

NERISSA.

Come, good sir, will you show me to this house?

[*Exeunt*.

15 **mayst**：can. **warrant**：assure you. **have**：hear. **old**：much，ample.

17 **outface**：put out of countenance，使窘迫。 **outswear**：exceed in swearing.

18 **tarry**：stay，wait.

ACT V

SCENE I

Belmont. Avenue to PORTIA'S *house.*

Enter LORENZO *and* JESSICA.

LORENZO.

The moon shines bright:—in such a night as this,
When the sweet wind did gently kiss the trees,
And they did make no noise,—in such a night
Troilus methinks mounted the Troyan walls,
And sigh'd his soul toward the Grecian tents,
Where Cressid lay that night.

JESSICA.

In such a night
Did Thisbe fearfully o'ertrip the dew,
And saw the lion's shadow ere himself,
And ran dismay'd away.

LORENZO.

In such a night
Stood Dido with a willow in her hand
Upon the wild sea-banks, and waft her love
To come again to Carthage.

JESSICA.

In such a night
Medea gather'd the enchanted herbs
That did renew old Aeson.

LORENZO.

In such a night
Did Jessica steal from the wealthy Jew,
And with an unthrift love did run from Venice

V.i

1 **in**: during (下同)。

4 **Troilus**[ˈtrɔiləs]: 特洛伊王子之一,和 Cressida[ˈkresidə]相爱, Cressida 的父亲 Calchas 早已逃到希腊军营中,为希腊人服务,后来 Cressida 以交换战俘方式回到希腊方面军营中她父亲处,并变了心。故事见乔叟的有关长诗和莎士比亚的有关剧本。 **Troyan**[ˈtrəujən]: 特洛伊的,平常作 Trojan.

5 **Grecian**[ˈgriːʃən]: 希腊的。

6 **Cressid**[ˈkresid]: 即 Cressida.

7 **Thisbe**[ˈθizbi]: 巴比伦女郎,她在去和青年 Pyramus[ˈpirəməs]幽会时被狮子吓跑,掉落面纱。Pyramus 来到幽会地点,看到狮子血嘴玷污的面纱,误以为 Thisbe 已死,立即自刎。Thisbe 从躲藏的地方出来,看见 Pyramus 已死,也跟着自杀。故事见莎士比亚《仲夏夜之梦》。 **o'ertrip**: run over.

8 **ere himself**: before it (itself).

9 **dismay'd**: confused by fear.

10 **Dido**[ˈdaidəu]: 迦太基女王爱上了逃避风浪而来的特洛伊王的驸马 Aeneas[iˈniːæs], 后者终于离弃她而去,她悲极而自焚。 **willow**: willow branch, symbol of forsaken love.

11 **waft**: wafted, waved to. **love**: lover.

13 **Medea**[miˈdiə]: Jason 之妻(见 I. i 170—172 行),她会魔术,曾在月夜采药,使公公 Aeson[ˈisən]返老还童。

14 **renew**: restore one's youth.

16 **unthrift**: prodigal, good-for-nothing.

As far as Belmont.

JESSICA.

In such a night
Did young Lorenzo swear he loved her well,
Stealing her soul with many vows of faith,
And ne'er a true one.

LORENZO.

In such a night
Did pretty Jessica, like a little shrew,
Slander her love, and he forgave it her.

JESSICA.

I would out-night you, did no body come:
But, hark, I hear the footing of a man.

Enter STEPHANO.

LORENZO.

Who comes so fast in silence of the night?

STEPHANO.

A friend.

LORENZO.

A friend! what friend? your name, I pray you, friend?

STEPHANO.

Stephano is my name; and I bring word
My mistress will before the break of day
Be here at Belmont: she doth stray about
By holy crosses, where she kneels and prays
For happy wedlock hours.

LORENZO.

Who comes with her?

STEPHANO.

None but a holy hermit and her maid.
I pray you, is my master yet return'd?

LORENZO.

He is not, nor we have not heard from him.—
But go we in, I pray thee, Jessica,

21 shrew：泼妇，悍妇。

22 love：lover.

23 out-night：outstrip you in this contest of making sentences beginning with "in such a night." **did no body come**：if nobody should come.

24 hark：listen. **footing**：footsteps.

25 in silence of：in the silence of.

30—31 doth…crosses：makes pilgrimages from one sacred shrine to another.

And ceremoniously let us prepare
Some welcome for the mistress of the house.

Enter LAUNCELOT.

LAUNCELOT GOBBO.

Sola, sola! wo ha, ho! sola, sola!

LORENZO.

Who calls?

LAUNCELOT GOBBO.

Sola! —did you see Master Lorenzo? Master Lorenzo! —sola, sola!

LORENZO.

Leave hollaing, man:—here.

LAUNCELOT GOBBO.

Sola! —where? where?

LORENZO.

Here.

LAUNCELOT GOBBO.

Tell him there's a post come from my master, with his horn full of good news: my master will be here ere morning. [*Exit*.

LORENZO.

Sweet soul, let's in, and there expect their coming.
And yet no matter:—why should we go in? —
My friend Stephano, signify, I pray you,
Within the house, your mistress is at hand;
And bring your music forth into the air.[*Exit* STEPHANO.
How sweet the moonlight sleeps upon this bank!
Here will we sit, and let the sounds of music
Creep in our ears: soft stillness and the night
Become the touches of sweet harmony.
Sit, Jessica. Look, how the floor of heaven
Is thick inlaid with patines of bright gold:
There's not the smallest orb which thou behold'st
But in his motion like an angel sings,

37 **ceremoniously**：修饰 prepare.

39 **sola**：hallo.

43 **Leave**：stop.

46 **post**：messenger.

49 **expect**：await.

50 **no matter**：it doesn't matter.

51 **signify**：give notice；announce.

52 **your mistress**：前省略 that.

53 **music**：乐队。 **into the air**：out-of-doors.

56 **in**：into.

57 **Become**：befit，accord with. **touches**：touchings on musical instruments；phrases.

59 **patines**：small plates (dishes) of metal 指星星。

60—61 **There's…sings**：旧时认为星辰运行时发出音乐。 **But**：that does not. **his**：its.

Still quiring to the young-eyed cherubins,—
Such harmony is in immortal souls;
But whilst this muddy vesture of decay
Doth grossly close it in, we cannot hear it.

Enter MUSICIANS.

Come, ho, and wake Diana with a hymn!
With sweetest touches pierce your mistress' ear,
And draw her home with music. [*Music plays*.

JESSICA.

I am never merry when I hear sweet music.

LORENZO.

The reason is, your spirits are attentive:
For do but note a wild and wanton herd,
Or race of youthful and unhandled colts,
Fetching mad bounds, bellowing, and neighing loud,
Which is the hot condition of their blood;
If they but hear perchance a trumpet sound,
Or any air of music touch their ears,
You shall perceive them make a mutual stand,
Their savage eyes turn'd to a modest gaze,
By the sweet power of music: therefore the poet
Did feign that Orpheus drew trees, stones, and floods;
Since naught so stockish, hard, and full of rage,
But music for the time doth change his nature.
The man that hath no music in himself,
Nor is not moved with concord of sweet sounds,
Is fit for treasons, stratagems, and spoils;
The motions of his spirit are dull as night,
And his affections dark as Erebus:
Let no such man be trusted.—Mark the music.

Enter PORTIA *and* NERISSA.

PORTIA.

That light we see is burning in my hall.
How far that little candle throws his beams!

62 **Still**：all the time. **quiring**：choiring，singing. **cherubins**：cherubs，小天使。

64 **muddy**：earthy. **vesture**：clothing(据认为人是上帝用土造成)。 **of decay**：mortal.

65 **grossly**：coarsely，rudely. **it**：指 harmony.

66 **Diana**：罗马神话中的月亮女神，象征贞洁。

68 **draw**：attract.

71 **note**：notice. **wanton**：frolicsome.

72 **race**：breed. **unhandled**：unbroken，未驯服的。 **colts**：小马驹。

73 **Fetching**：making，taking (speaking of motions). **mad**：wild. **bounds**：leaps.

75 **perchance**：by chance.

77 **mutual**：common. **make…stand**：all stand still at the same time.

78 **turn'd**：changed (与 savage eyes 构成独立主格结构)。**modest**：restrained，tamed，驯顺的。

79 **the poet**：指希腊诗人 Ovid (43 B.C. —c.17 A.D.).

80 **feign**：invent the tale. **Orpheus**[ˈɔːfjuːs]：希腊神话中音乐之神，他的乐器是一种手持的七弦竖琴 lyre. **drew**：attracted.

81 **naught**：(there is) nothing. **stockish**：wooden，stolid. **rage**：savage disposition.

84 **moved with**：moved by. **concord**：harmony.

85 **stratagems**：deeds of violence. **spoils**：acts of plundering.

87 **affections**：passions. **Erebus**[ˈeribəs]：希腊神话中鬼魂到阴府去所经过的地下黑暗区域。

90 **his**：its.

So shines a good deed in a naughty world.

NERISSA.

When the moon shone, we did not see the candle.

PORTIA.

So doth the greater glory dim the less:
A substitute shines brightly as a king,
Until a king be by; and then his state
Empties itself, as doth an inland brook
Into the main of waters.—Music! hark!

NERISSA.

It is your music, madam, of the house.

PORTIA.

Nothing is good, I see, without respect:
Methinks it sounds much sweeter than by day.

NERISSA.

Silence bestows that virtue on it, madam.

PORTIA.

The crow doth sing as sweetly as the lark,
When neither is attended; and I think
The nightingale, if she should sing by day,
When every goose is cackling, would be thought
No better a musician than the wren.
How many things by season season'd are
To their right praise and true perfection! —
Peace, ho! the moon sleeps with Endymion,
And would not be awaked. [*Music ceases*.

LORENZO.

That is the voice,
Or I am much deceived, of Portia.

PORTIA.

He knows me, as the blind man knows the cuckoo,
By the bad voice.

LORENZO.

Dear lady, welcome home.

91 **naughty**：wicked，evil.

93 **the less**：the lesser glory.

94 **substitute**：deputy，代表，代替者。 **brightly**：前省略 as.

95 **state**：pomp，splendour.

97 **main of waters**：sea.

98 **your music**：你的乐队。

99 **without respect**：without reference to circumstances.

103 **attended**：attended to，accompanied，旁边有别的鸟在叫。

106 **wren**：鹪鹩。

107 **by season**：by appearing at the suitable time，by timeliness，由于时机合适。 **season'd are/To**：are qualified for.

108 **right**：deserved，应得的。

109 **Peace**：Keep quiet. **Endymion**[enˈdimĭən]：希腊神话中年轻美貌的牧羊人。月亮女神 Diana 垂爱于他，每在他睡着时来拥抱他。济慈有长诗专写他的故事。

111 **Or**：otherwise.

PORTIA.

We have been praying for our husbands' health,
Which speed, we hope, the better for our words.
Are they return'd?

LORENZO.

Madam, they are not yet;
But there is come a messenger before,
To signify their coming.

PORTIA.

Go in, Nerissa;
Give orders to my servants that they take
No note at all of our being absent hence;—
Nor you, Lorenzo;—Jessica, nor you.

[*A tucket sounds*.

LORENZO.

Your husband is at hand; I hear his trumpet:
We are no tell-tales, madam; fear you not.

PORTIA.

This night methinks is but the daylight sick;
It looks a little paler: 'tis a day,
Such as the day is when the sun is hid.

Enter BASSAIO, ANTONIO, GRATIANO, *and their* FOLLOWERS.

BASSANIO.

We should hold day with the Antipodes,
If you would walk in absence of the sun.

PORTIA.

Let me give light, but let me not be light;
For a light wife doth make a heavy husband,
And never be Bassanio so for me:
But God sort all! —You're welcome home, my lord.

BASSANIO.

I thank you, madam. Give welcome to my friend:
This is the man, this is Antonio,
To whom I am so infinitely bound.

115 speed：prosper.

119—120 take/No note：不要提到。

tucket：a short flourish on the trumpet，喇叭花腔。

127 Antipodes[æn'tipədiːz]：地球背面。 **We… Antipodes**：我们会和地球背面的人同时过白天(i.e. have daylight at night).

128 If…sun：because your beauty shines like the sun，your presence makes darkness light.

129 前一 **light**(n.)：光明。后一 **light**(adj.)：轻佻的。

130 light；heavy：这两个词都是双关语：light 1.轻的；2.轻佻的。heavy 1.重的；2.忧愁的 (heavy-hearted).

132 sort：ordain，dispose，注定，安排。 **God sort all!**：(祈愿用语)上帝做主！上帝赐福！

135 bound：obliged.

PORTIA.
You should in all sense be much bound to him,
For, as I hear, he was much bound for you.

ANTONIO.
No more than I am well acquitted of.

PORTIA.
Sir, you are very welcome to our house:
It must appear in other ways than words,
Therefore I scant this breathing courtesy.

GRATIANO [*to* NERISSA].
By yonder moon I swear you do me wrong;
In faith, I gave it to the judge's clerk:
Would he were gelt that had it, for my part,
Since you do take it, love, so much at heart.

PORTIA.
A quarrel, ho, already! what's the matter?

GRATIANO.
About a hoop of gold, a paltry ring
That she did give to me; whose posy was
For all the world like cutler's poetry
Upon a knife, 'Love me, and leave me not.'

NERISSA.
What talk you of the posy or the value?
You swore to me, when I did give it you,
That you would wear it till your hour of death;
And that it should lie with you in your grave:
Though not for me, yet for your vehement oaths,
You should have been respective, and have kept it.
Gave it a judge's clerk! no, God's my judge,
The clerk will ne'er wear hair on's face that had it.

GRATIANO.
He will, an if he live to be a man.

NERISSA.
Ay, if a woman live to be a man.

136 sense：reason.

137 was much bound：undertook a grave responsibility，承担严重责任。

138 acquitted of：released from，解脱。

141 scant：cut short. **breathing courtesy**：courteous talk.

144 gelt：gelded，阉割。

147 paltry：worthless.

148 posy：motto engraved on the inside of a ring.

149 For all the world：(表强调)completely.

156 respective：careful.

157 a judge's clerk：前面省略 to. **God's my judge**：God is my judge，上帝为证。

158 hair：beard.

GRATIANO.

Now, by this hand, I gave it to a youth,—
A kind of boy; a little scrubbed boy,
No higher than thyself, the judge's clerk;
A prating boy, that begg'd it as a fee:
I could not for my heart deny it him.

PORTIA.

You were to blame,—I must be plain with you,—
To part so slightly with your wife's first gift;
A thing stuck on with oaths upon your finger,
And so riveted with faith unto your flesh.
I gave my love a ring, and made him swear
Never to part with it; and here he stands,—
I dare be sworn for him, he would not leave it,
Nor pluck it from his finger, for the wealth
That the world masters. Now, in faith, Gratiano,
You give your wife too unkind a cause of grief:
An 'twere to me, I should be mad at it.

BASSANIO [*aside*].

Why, I were best to cut my left hand off,
And swear I lost the ring defending it.

GRATIANO.

My Lord Bassanio gave his ring away
Unto the judge that begg'd it, and indeed
Deserved it too; and then the boy, his clerk,
That took some pains in writing, he begg'd mine:
And neither man nor master would take aught
But the two rings.

PORTIA.

What ring gave you, my lord?
Not that, I hope, which you received of me.

BASSANIO.

If I could add a lie unto a fault,
I would deny it; but you see my finger

161 **by**：I swear by.
162 **scrubbed**：像灌木(scrub)一样矮小的。
164 **prating**：babbling，爱讲话的。 **fee**：reward.
165 **for my heart**：(强调语)for my life，无论如何。
166 **plain**：frank.
168 **stuck on**：attached，fastened.
169 **riveted**：fastened strongly，as if with rivets (铆钉)。
174 **masters**：is master of，possesses.
176 **mad**：furious.
177 **I were best**：It would have been better for me.

Hath not the ring upon it,—it is gone.

PORTIA.

Even so void is your false heart of truth.
By heaven, I will ne'er come in your bed
Until I see the ring.

NERISSA.

Nor I in yours
Till I again see mine.

BASSANIO.

Sweet Portia,
If you did know to whom I gave the ring,
If you did know for whom I gave the ring,
And would conceive for what I gave the ring,
And how unwillingly I left the ring,
When naught would be accepted but the ring,
You would abate the strength of your displeasure.

PORTIA.

If you had known the virtue of the ring,
Or half her worthiness that gave the ring,
Or your own honour to contain the ring,
You would not then have parted with the ring.
What man is there so much unreasonable,
If you had pleased to have defended it
With any terms of zeal, wanted the modesty
To urge the thing held as a ceremony?
Nerissa teaches me what to believe:
I'll die for't but some woman had the ring.

BASSANIO.

No, by my honour, madam, by my soul,
No woman had it, but a civil doctor,
Which did refuse three thousand ducats of me,
And begg'd the ring; the which I did deny him,
And suffer'd him to go displeased away;
Even he that did uphold the very life

195 **conceive**: understand.

196 **left**: parted with.

199 **virtue**: power.

200 **her worthiness that**: the worthiness of her who.

201 **contain**: keep.

203 **so much**: so.

204 If it had pleased you to defend the ring with any zeal, who would be so unreasonable as to lack the prudence and demand it which is considered a sacred token?

205 **wanted**: who lacked. **modesty**: prudence.

206 **urge**: demand. **ceremony**: sacred pledge，神圣的信物。

208 **I'll…but**: I'll wager my life on it that….

210 **civil doctor**: doctor of civil law, lawyer.

211 **Which**: who.

213 **suffered…go**: let him go.

214 **uphold**: save by defending.

Of my dear friend. What should I say, sweet lady?
I was enforced to send it after him:
I was beset with shame and courtesy;
My honour would not let ingratitude
So much besmear it. Pardon me, good lady;
For, by these blessed candles of the night,
Had you been there, I think, you would have begg'd
The ring of me to give the worthy doctor.

PORTIA.

Let not that doctor e'er come near my house:
Since he hath got the jewel that I loved,
And that which you did swear to keep for me,
I will become as liberal as you;
I'll not deny him any thing I have,
No, not my body nor my husband's bed:
Know him I shall, I am well sure of it:
Lie not a night from home; watch me like Argus:
If you do not, if I be left alone,
Now, by mine honour, which is yet mine own,
I'll have that doctor for my bedfellow.

NERISSA.

And I his clerk; therefore be well advised
How you do leave me to mine own protection.

GRATIANO.

Well, do you so: let not me take him, then;
For if I do, I'll mar the young clerk's pen.

ANTONIO.

I am the unhappy subject of these quarrels.

PORTIA.

Sir, grieve not you; you are welcome notwithstanding.

BASSANIO.

Portia, forgive me this enforced wrong;
And, in the hearing of these many friends,
I swear to thee, even by thine own fair eyes,

216 **enforced**：constrained.
217 **courtesy**：obligation of courtesy，欠礼之感。
219 **besmear**：smear，stain.
220 **blessed candles**：stars.
229 **Know**：have sexual intercourse with.
230 **Argus**[ˈɑːgəs]：希腊神话中担任警卫的百眼怪。
234 **be well advised**：be warned.
237 **pen**：兼有 penis 的双关义。
240 **enforced wrong**：this wrong thing I was forced to do.

Wherein I see myself,—

PORTIA.

Mark you but that!
In both my eyes he doubly sees himself;
In each eye, one:—swear by your double self,
And there's an oath of credit.

BASSANIO.

Nay, but hear me:
Pardon this fault, and by my soul I swear
I never more will break an oath with thee.

ANTONIO.

I once did lend my body for his wealth;
Which, but for him that had your husband's ring,
Had quite miscarried: I dare be bound again,
My soul upon the forfeit, that your lord
Will never more break faith advisedly.

PORTIA.

Then you shall be his surety. Give him this;
And bid him keep it better than the other.

ANTONIO.

Here, Lord Bassanio; swear to keep this ring.

BASSANIO.

By heaven, it is the same I gave the doctor!

PORTIA.

I had it of him; pardon me, Bassanio;
For, by this ring, the doctor lay with me.

NERISSA.

And pardon me, my gentle Gratiano;
For that same scrubbed boy, the doctor's clerk,
In lieu of this, last night did lie with me.

GRATIANO.

Why, this is like the mending of highways
In summer, where the ways are fair enough:
What, are we cuckolds ere we have deserved it?

244 doubly sees himself: see himself as two men (as a double face).

245 double: deceitful.

246 an…credit: (ironical) an oath that may be believed (i.e. that can't be believed at all).

249 wealth: welfare, prosperity.

250 Which: my body. **him that**: the person who.

251 Had: would have. **miscarried**: perished. **be bound**: 立下契约。

252 upon the forfeit: as security, 作为担保。

253 advisedly: on purpose, deliberately.

258 of: from.

259 by:凭借。 **lay**: slept.

262 In lieu of: in return for.

263—264 Why,…enough: 像夏季修理畅通无阻的大路(意即妻子在与他们同房以前已经不贞)。

PORTIA.

Speak not so grossly.—You are all amazed:
Here is a letter, read it at your leisure;
It comes from Padua, from Bellario:
There you shall find that Portia was the doctor;
Nerissa there her clerk: Lorenzo here
Shall witness I set forth as soon as you,
And even but now return'd; I have not yet
Enter'd my house.—Antonio, you are welcome;
And I have better news in store for you
Than you expect: unseal this letter soon;
There you shall find three of your argosies
Are richly come to harbour suddenly:
You shall not know by what strange accident
I chanced on this letter.

ANTONIO.

I am dumb.

BASSANIO.

Were you the doctor, and I knew you not?

GRATIANO.

Were you the clerk that is to make me cuckold?

NERISSA.

Ay, but the clerk that never means to do it,
Unless he live until he be a man.

BASSANIO.

Sweet doctor, you shall be my bedfellow:
When I am absent, then lie with my wife.

ANTONIO.

Sweet lady, you have given me life and living;
For here I read for certain that my ships
Are safely come to road.

PORTIA.

How now, Lorenzo!
My clerk hath some good comforts too for you.

271 **witness**： bear witness.

272 **even but now**： just now.

279 **dumb**： speechless with wonder.

282 **but the clerk**： but I was the clerk.

286 **living**： property， means of living.

288 **road**： roads， anchorage.

289 **comforts**： good things.

NERISSA.

Ay, and I'll give them him without a fee.—
There do I give to you and Jessica,
From the rich Jew, a special deed of gift,
After his death, of all he dies possest of.

LORENZO.

Fair ladies, you drop manna in the way
Of starved people.

PORTIA.

It is almost morning,
And yet I am sure you are not satisfied
Of these events at full. Let us go in;
And charge us there upon inter'gatories,
And we will answer all things faithfully.

GRATIANO.

Let it be so: the first inter'gatory
That my Nerissa shall be sworn on is,
Whether till the next night she had rather stay,
Or go to bed now, being two hours to day:
But were the day come, I should wish it dark,
That I were couching with the doctor's clerk.
Well, while I live I'll fear no other thing
So sore as keeping safe Nerissa's ring. [*Exeunt*.

294 **manna**：吗哪(古犹太人经过旷野时，从天而降的神赐食物，见《圣经·旧约·出埃及记》第16章14节以下)。

297 **Of**：with.

298 **charge us**：question us under oath. **upon inter'gatories**：按照讯问表上所列的问题。

303 **day**：daybreak.

305 **couching**：sleeping.

306 **fear**：be anxious about.

307 **sore**：intensely. **ring**：兼有女性生殖器的双关义。

图书在版编目(CIP)数据

威尼斯商人 /(英)莎士比亚(Shakespeare, W.)著;张文庭注释.—北京:商务印书馆,2014(2016.3 重印)
(莎翁戏剧经典)
ISBN 978-7-100-09896-0

Ⅰ. ①威… Ⅱ. ①莎… ②张… Ⅲ. ①英语—语言读物 ②剧本—英国—中世纪 Ⅳ. ①H319.4:I

中国版本图书馆 CIP 数据核字(2013)第 072226 号

莎翁戏剧经典
WĒINÍSĪ SHĀNGRÉN
威 尼 斯 商 人
〔英〕威廉·莎士比亚 著
张文庭 注释

商 务 印 书 馆 出 版
(北京王府井大街36号 邮政编码 100710)
商 务 印 书 馆 发 行
北 京 冠 中 印 刷 厂 印 刷
ISBN 978-7-100-09896-0

2014 年 8 月第 1 版　　开本 787×1092 1/32
2016 年 3 月北京第 2 次印刷　　印张 7¾ 插页 1
定价:26.00 元

I was a pair of boots I wouldn't have to beg I'd be closer, closer to you Closer, yo

It takes so many steps I pretend that I'm a tick to attached Just being around your

closer, closer to you If I was a necklace Hanging decorate your lips Closer, closer

when you want Wish I was a wicked shot Draped down your front When you fe

ned Closer, closer, closer to you Closer closer closer to round your bed Right next

to you Each and everyday Closer, closer closer to you If I had my wishes If I

you move around I'd see you walking by Closer Wish I was a stocking Clo

I was a pair of boots I wouldn't have to beg I'd be closer, closer to you Closer, yo

Wishes a many cups I pretend that I'm a kid It satisfied Just being round yo

get closer closer to you If I were a necklace Hanging decorate your lips Closer clo

what you want Wish I was a naked fire Draped down your front When you

unt Closer closer closer to you Closer closer closer to round your bed Right ne

er to you Each and everyday Closer closer closer to you If I had my wishes If

e you move around I'd view you walking by Closer Wish I was a stocking C

I was a pair of boots I wouldn't have to beg I'd be closer closer to you Closer